RAZOR EDGE

A PARKER McINTYRE

NOVEL

By Rodney Shields

Table of Contents

Prologue

Phsst.....Phsst... Her muffled scream of pain echoed among the rocky, tree-strewn mountainside. Piercing through the dusk-laden sky, it was audibly low, yet hauntingly subdued and controlled, as if not wanting to alert anyone. I quickly turned and was knocked backwards, tumbling downward, my body out of control, accelerating, arms flailing, clawing, reaching for something to hold on to, something to stop the fall. Momentary blackness, hardness, confusion, and then stopping...

Pain shot out from under my left side as I remained motionless, wedged awkwardly against a fallen tree trunk. Phsst....Phsst... two more shots rang out, kicking up dirt above where I had just tumbled from. No time to think. Reacting quickly, I looked in the direction I thought the shots came from and worked quickly to free myself from the clutches of the tree.

Scrambling forward on my knees, I pushed my torn and battered body up into a small cavity surrounded by trees that I prayed would protect me. "Okay, assess, find a solution fast," I whispered, breathing hard and wiping a blinding wetness from my eyes. I was worrying about Kelly as my thoughts cleared. Her last known location was up there.

Looking back up the slope, I saw that my tumble was no more than about fifty feet or so, not as bad as it felt. Taking inventory of myself quickly, I found that I was bleeding from a small cut above my right eye, and my nosebleed had stopped from the earlier beating. Nothing felt broken, although my adrenaline was running on high alert. I could feel my muscles throbbing and starting to stiffen up. Hell, I hurt! Wiping the blood from my cheek with my shirt sleeve, I sat thinking, okay, now what?

A few hours ago, the evening had an alluring dusky sky here in the Utah High Uintas wilderness of the Ashley National Forest. But now it had given way to a darkness so black and intense that the stars were struggling to illuminate it. The cabin was another sixty feet down and east of me, and I could almost feel the heat of its lights and the dangers it held. We were on the Green River close to the Flaming Gorge Reservoir, not far from the Wyoming line. The majestic views of Bear Peak, Painters Peak, Mt. Davis, and Kings Peak—the highest in the Uintas at 13,528 feet—seemed like a distant memory from my present location down one of the Gorge's many canyons and divides.

"Shit!" I snorted. I hadn't seen this coming. "Focus, damn it, and assess the situation!" I said again, willing myself to do something. Find his location and eradicate the problem. Draw him out! Damn it! Phsst......Phsst.... Two more shots above me and to the right. Alright, I can't stay here. I've got to move up the slope to the tree line; that would be the best option right now. The cabin was eerily quiet, and at any moment, someone was going to notice me out here in the open.

Surprisingly, I still held on to the SIG P228 with a Viridiax laser sight that I had taken from Marko. Unfortunately, this would not be effective. Phsst......Phsst.....Phsst. Three more shots off target and from the opposite direction. I assumed that the shooter was across the river behind the cover of the rocks or in the lower tree line, which would give him a great sightline at us to the west. But then again, if he was on this side of the gorge in the forested area southeast of my current position, he would still have a great line of sight. But... It didn't matter, I thought. Chaos!

Chapter 1

Friday, 46 miles southeast of downtown Cleveland at West Branch State Park in Ravenna, Ohio, a dark, lean, and fit man turned onto the Lakeside Trail.

Pedal, coast, pedal, breathe, breathe, pedal, breathe, relax! Hit it hard now and dig, dig...!

Exuding confidence on his bike, he started to accelerate up the hill, blinded by adrenaline. The Lakeside Trail, with its comfortable array of beech, maple, and cucumber magnolia trees, snakes up and down and around, in and out of beautiful water-lined coves. It's actually 12 miles of badass, hardcore, lung-burning, mountain bike single track, right smack dab in the middle of central Portage County. Not more than a one-hour drive from the high-rise confines of the burning river city on the south banks of Lake Erie, the park is a hidden jewel that surrounds 2,650 acres of pristine blue lake that people flock to daily for all types of outdoor recreation and relaxation.

Ping vibrate, ping vibrate. Ignoring the sound and the feeling, the lone rider continued to pedal, climb, dig! Dig! Whatever it was, the trails were empty of their normal clank and bang of mountain bikes swooping through the canopy of trees and steep, relentless valleys. Ping vibrates again. He heard the annoying little tone in his ear. Reaching up, right hand off the handlebar, he quickly and carefully tapped the small button on the earpiece.

"Hello!...............you there?" The voice, nervous and quick, awaited a response. He paused, breathing rapidly, and said nothing. Cresting the hill, he then started to descend, concentrating only on the terrain in front of him. In the zone, anticipation building, the feeling... life was good, while you had it.

Tapping his ear again, the call ended, and not a word was spoken from the man known as "the Tool." Reaching the other side of the small valley at the precise time required would take some effort, and he didn't need interruptions. It was muggy, hot, and the small distractions, along with the heat flying around him in the form of small buzzing insects, were starting to weigh on his mindset. Breathing extremely hard for this first section, he thought his fitness level had not been serving him well lately. A change in his fitness regimen was going to be needed, he thought.

It would take him at least 30 minutes at a medium anaerobic pace to cover the distance and have enough time to set up. The Tool was only 10 minutes into this one, 20 more left. Stopping for water on a bluff overlooking the beautiful blue azure waters of the West Branch Reservoir, he could understand why people liked to flock to this state park for relaxation. The earpiece beeped. "Damn..." He huffed and tapped. "..........she is here and waiting." The voice echoed.

Severely bothered by the unnecessary interruption by this fool that he was working for, he spoke for the first time after leaving his rental car across the lake. "Okay... it will be done, rest assured, my friend," the Tool said in a cool, smooth, slightly accented voice. Turning the bike around a large mud hole in the trail—one must protect the environment, he thought—he continued to ride at a feverish pace. Pedal, pedal, climb, climb, breathe... dig... pedal, relax, thinking about his exit plan and the distance to his car across the lake.

Chapter 2

"Hot! Hot! Freaking hot!" Guy sang as he sped down Newton Falls Rd, heading towards a date of riding mountain bikes and hopefully hanging out afterward with an attractive woman named Laurie.

The temperature was in the mid-nineties with high humidity and a chance of rain.

"Shit! A damn shower might screw up this date at any minute; that would be my luck," he thought.

Guy was so immersed in the thought of his date with beautiful Laurie Rice, he almost missed Rock Springs Rd. This date with Laurie Rice had been set up two weeks ago, but due to conflicts in their schedules, it was almost canceled. The government projects he worked closely on demanded a lot of calculated time, and if for some reason, any reason, they felt that he and the company were not fulfilling their end of the contract, the plug would be pulled and lots of money and future contracts could be lost. Not a good prospect, no, not good at all. So the date was set for today, Friday! She had said, "Be there or be square, rain or shine."

Laurie is a co-worker of his at Sys-tech Corporation in Ravenna. She works in the accounting department, and he is a senior technical design engineer. They would see each other daily as he moved from department to department, checking on the progress of important details pertaining to the projects he was working on. Guy had also learned through mutual friends that Laurie was into extreme and outdoor sports, especially biking. "Whoa... she's not only beautiful... she also loves danger... sign her up," he had said to a close friend at work. So, here he was, going to meet her for a ride and maybe dinner and drinks afterward. "Hell yes!... all is good," Guy thought and started singing again.

Turning his Honda Element into the West Branch State Park mountain bike trails parking lot, Guy saw Laurie standing at the rear of her Honda, unloading a sweet-looking Santa Cruz mountain bike. Her sun-streaked golden blonde hair was pulled back into a short ponytail, and she was wearing black baggy shorts and a white tank top that showed off her golden brown tan. The whole package was nice—long, lean, and muscular in an athletic sort of way. In the late afternoon light, Guy could see her transparent blue eyes dancing with the element of excitement and danger. Parking next to her car, Guy was out in a flash, stumbling as he leaped from the still-moving car.

"What's up, little lady?" he asked, grinning.

"Are you really ready to get your ass kicked?" she asked him, flashing that million-dollar smile.

"Please do, little lady," he said, smiling as if he had won the lottery, and maybe he did.

They finished unloading quickly, unaware of the watchful eyes upon them. The late summer afternoon was starting to haze up, and the damn deer flies were relentless as they applied repellant. Mounting their bikes and heading to the trailhead, Guy noticed that for a Friday afternoon, the parking lot seemed unusually empty, with the exception of one dark blue sedan.

"Everything good?" he asked Laurie as she checked over her bike.

"Yep," she replied, adjusting her helmet.

"Time to ride!" he said.

"I'll lead...come on, follow me, big guy," Laurie yelled, tearing off down the trail fast.

They sped out onto Gorge Rd Trail, fast and free, with Laurie leading and smiling. Turning onto the single track, they snaked back and forth between trees and sped up lung-burning climbs, enjoying the off-camber roots and rock-filled downhills as they completed the first 2.0 miles of what would be an exciting and fun ride. Stopping at the crossover at Cable Line Rd to eat an energy bar and drink some water, they discussed whether to ride the expert section that leads into the Rock Wall Trail or continue on the Lakeside Trail.

Chapter 3

Porterville, PA: "Parker, move your hands to the right just a tad!" Ken shouted up at me.

"Faauck!" I exclaimed. "Can't get it, dude!" I tried to hook a small rock with my index finger and thumb, missing it entirely and deadpanning the move.

My name is Parker McIntyre, and I am a private investigator who, at this moment, is about to start a free fall towards an impending ass ache 50 feet below onto some jagged rocks and the relatively shallow riverbed of the Slippery Rock River. Only this will not happen today because Ken Peterson, my climbing partner and best friend, will hopefully tighten his grip on the rope, causing the Trick Research belaying device to lock up and forcefully stop me from dropping any further than the three feet I already have.

The rock wall that we are climbing is called Mission Impossible and is located in the far northwestern corner of McConnell's Mill State Park, a really nice area for bouldering and rock climbing. True to its name, our mission today seems impossible.

"P-Mac! I think we can safely agree that this would be a good time to wrap this one up," Ken said tiredly, belaying. We could hear a dog barking excitedly above us in the near distance, and I thought of Bark, my dog. Bark had gone on all my short climbing trips, but not today; he was kind of under the weather.

"Well, okay, cool. Let's hike up to the road instead of climbing out, and then we can grab the ropes. And hell, I'll even treat you to lunch," I said, smiling.

"Deal!" responded Ken.

"Yeah, he would agree so long as he wasn't buying," I thought.

We gathered up our gear and stopped off at the Bagel Hut to purchase a couple of sun-dried turkey pesto wraps and raspberry iced tea. Sitting down on a bench, we basked in the late evening heat, drenched with excitement from the climb and the sweltering humidity. We ate and talked about the merits of using certain moves and techniques for the rock problems we had encountered today. I took my iPhone out and checked messages. I had two. Ken looked over my shoulder at the messages as he got up and laughed.

"Restroom cat," he said, walking away.

"What?" Ken said, returning from the restroom, looking at me.

"Tell you on the road. Let's go," I said.

Ken joined MRO as an investigator and partner after a five-year stint as a State Police officer following his graduation from law school.

"Callie has something for us, and Ant shot me a text," I replied, getting up and throwing our wrappers away

"Ant! What's up with him, man?" Ken asked, quizzical, scratching his blond buzz cut and squinting into the sun.

Turning around and shrugging my shoulders, hands out in a you-know kind of gesture, I picked up my phone. "Got him checking on some crap, Kenny boy," I said, walking toward the SUV

"Sounds heavy if you got him looking!" Ken said, grinning.

"Kinda like you..." I said, pointing to his midsection, which has seen considerable growth of late

Slightly offended, he replied curtly, "Screw you! It was this five-foot-eleven, two-hundred-pound man that saved you."

Laughing, I climbed into his vehicle and closed the door, shaking my head.

"Ghost involved?" he asked, trying to change the subject.

"Yeah... laughing... if I need my life saved by him and now you," I quipped.

"Shit! He'll appreciate saving it again... what's the count now?" Ken said, having fun with this.

"I don't necessarily want to talk about it."

"Okay, then let's roll. I am sure Callie wants to see you asap," smiled Ken.

"Yep, and I got a dog to feed. I hope he didn't get sick in the house," I said, biting my lower lip, emulating a snarl.

"How did you know she said asap?" I asked.

"She always does..." Ken laughed and turned out onto Old Forge Rd.

Your Highness Ann Callie Banner, my cousin, is the office manager at McIntyre, Reed & O'Brien, an upscale private investigative firm located in Westlake, Ohio, that I currently run. Callie, who is five years older than me, has always been more of an older sister than a cousin, so it's easy to see why she is the voice of reason at the firm, the real boss. MRO, as we are called, was started by my uncles Jim McIntyre and Cyrus Reed back in the late 1970s. I had taken over the day-to-day operations of MRO after an unfortunate and tragic backcountry hiking accident claimed the life of my uncle Jim. His body was never found. Uncle Cyrus is no longer in the game, having retired down to the Keys after Jim's death, citing that the time was right for enjoying life. Cyrus is Callie's father. So now he spends his time fishing and chasing rich divorcees around in the Keys. I think his real reasoning was not enjoying the fruits of his success and Jim's life being cut short.

Ant's message simply said, "Get back with me! Need to talk. I have some intel on your problem."

Tyrone "Ant" James works for another investigative firm in the downtown metro area of

Cleveland. He and his partner, a relative of mine who only goes by the name of Ghost, are good and resourceful friends. We have, in past years, worked cases jointly.

Callie's message was: Get a hold of me ASAP. Got an important thing for you.

Chapter 4

West Branch, 2.4 miles ahead on the Rock Wall trail, the Tool stops to take in the serene view. He dismounts his bike and leans it against a medium-sized beech maple tree, then walks silently around the trail, checking for other cyclists.

His slow, methodical gait and intense, emotionless expression make him appear disarming, almost boy-band-like. The Tool, as he's called, is an expert at solving problems, hired for his efficiency at a high price, with strict rules—no kids or mothers.

Breathing in the muggy air, he detaches himself from reality. Jobs like this can get messy fast. With a debt to pay, he's here reluctantly. The people pulling the strings insisted he handle it personally.

"Debt paid!" he muses, smirking. "Let's get through these kills and see where I stand. Then I'll deal with those little shits later." He smiles at the thought.

He refocuses, staring at the wooded area before him, covered in woodland flowers. The excitement of life, death, and tranquility grips him. Power, he thinks—to take and to give—shatters the tranquility and makes him pause. He trips on uneven ground but catches himself, murmuring, "Refocus."

A sharp descent to the right catches his eye. The drop is about 40 feet into a small bowl with deadfall covering the bottom. "Hmm, this will do nicely," he thinks, swatting a fly. Another five-foot drop to a small ditch intrigues him.

Climbing down, he surveys the bottom, thinking it would make a perfect body dump. The bodies will be found, given the woodland creatures and biking traffic. "Bodies fall, no vision at all...one way in, no way out," he murmurs.

Smirking, he climbs back to his bike. Absorbed in the view, he doesn't notice his cell phone pinging until it stops. Tapping his ear, he listens.

Chapter 5

PA. Turning onto Old Forge Rd, we hit a traffic jam. State Police and Park Rangers were helping cars turn around. A crowd gathered near a crime scene taped-off area, while emergency vehicles and squad cars blocked local TV crews.

Ken buzzed his driver side window down and asked a passing teenager, "Excuse me, Sir, what's going on up there?"

"A woman's remains were found in the woods by the pavilion," the kid replied, pointing.

"Damn! What happened?" Ken asked.

"Dunno. A dude and his girlfriend found her. It was the dog that found her."

"Whew, harsh. Thanks," Ken said, reaching the officer turning traffic around.

"Damn!" I said.

"Yeah," Ken replied, shaking his head.

We turned the SUV around and followed the traffic out of the park. After a 15-minute detour, we were on interstate 79, heading north towards the PA turnpike. Grooving to "If I had eyes" by Jack Johnson, I couldn't stop thinking about the woman's body. It was unnerving, remembering my uncle's situation.

"I don't believe Big Jim's death was an accident," I said.

"Yeah, I heard you were inquiring about it," Ken said.

"What do you think?"

"Nothing really. We need more intel. It could be something else, or just an accident."

"Do you think I'm crazy for pursuing this?" I asked.

"No, but we need to find out what really happened in Green River," Ken said.

"It's a delicate situation. It might open old wounds with Callie," I responded.

"True, but we should take a logical approach and look at it from all angles," Ken added.

"True," I smiled.

Ken paid the turnpike toll and accelerated towards the Ohio border. He turned to look at me. "Callie's not going to like this when she finds out," he said, waiting for a response but getting none.

"I think he's involved," I said, staring ahead.

"You mean Holtz, right?" Ken replied.

"Yep, that's my observation," Ken said softly. "Given their relationship, something must have happened."

"Yeah, I've come to realize that."

"So, welcome to my reality," I said.

"You own a successful investigative firm," Ken added.

Ken's car Bluetooth alerted him to a call. "Did you not think my message was important?" Before I could answer, she said, "Hi, Kenneth."

It was my cousin's voice through the car speakers. "Hello, Cal!" Ken responded.

"That's Callie, not Cal," she corrected.

"Okay," he said, grinning.

"Parker, you have work to do. Mr. Schaefer has been calling relentlessly," she said.

"I thought his case was handled?" I replied.

"It was, with help from Little John and Styles," I added, sharing the blame.

"Styles was involved?" she asked incredulously.

"Yes, Callie," I said, sensing her concern.

"Pretty boy," I mumbled.

"Oh crap, there's the problem," she said, maybe hearing me.

"What's the issue with Mr. Schaefer?" I asked.

"Big Al thinks someone at the firm is having an affair with his wife," she said sarcastically.

We burst out laughing.

"Tell you later," I said.

Chapter 6

Avon, Ohio. "Son of a bitch!" Jonas snorted, wiping sweat from his brow as he watched his putt drift away from the cup. The warm morning had turned temperate, disrupting his plans.

These two guys can't play golf, but they just delivered a load of cash to his offshore account. Jonas could endure them until they delivered the package.

"What country are you from?" Jonas asked, grabbing a water bottle.

"I didn't say, my sneaky American friend," the larger of the two replied, smiling.

Jonas Habbas, VP of Global Development & Operations at Sys-Tech Technologies, and his partner, Paul Lee Raverstine, were playing their weekly golf game. Today, they were entertaining two Eastern European businessmen with a business agenda.

The foursome was finishing their second round at the exclusive Avon Ledges Country Club, followed by dinner and a party in Gates Mills. SysTech Technologies, a global tech leader, had US headquarters in Hudson, Ohio, and Frederick, Maryland, with R&D locations in Green River, Wyoming, and Lake Charles, Louisiana.

Jonas, tall, slender, and handsome, was an Ivy League graduate with a brooding, planner's demeanor.

His blue-gray eyes were hidden behind expensive Tom Ford aviators. He exuded a sense of reckless cruelty.

Paul Lee, dark and wiry with a runner's build, contrasted Jonas. Raised and educated in Cambridge, he also had an Ivy League background.

"Well, gentlemen, it looks like I won't be joining the PGA tour this year," Jonas smiled, putting his putter away.

"I neither, Jonas, but it's not their luxury to have us," one man replied in good English.

A phone chirped, and everyone checked their waistbands, except Paul Lee, who had left his phone in the car.

"Excuse me, gents, I must take this call," Jonas said, stepping away.

"Hello, this better be good," he said, the smile fading into a mask of concern.

"Good, you've been busy," he said curtly, disconnecting. He hoped the damn fool handled the business at West Branch State Park.

Mickel Hernandez, known as the Tool, was a high-priced fixer with a wide client list. Efficient, quick, and clean, he was lethal but didn't touch mothers or children. Rumors said he worked for the government, though unconfirmed. He carefully put away his earpiece and listened.

Slipping off his water pack, the Tool pulled out a Kahr PM9 semi-automatic pistol and a custom-made silencer. Screwing the silencer onto the PM9, he marveled at its smooth, matte finish. Chambering a round, he felt the anticipation of the kill.

He moved across the trail, waiting and listening. "One way in, no way out," he repeated as he heard the cyclist approaching, wiping sweat from his mouth.

Chapter 7

Hours later, some 1,578 miles west and north at Mustang Ridge in Flaming Gorge Reservoir, Utah—northwest of Dutch John and about forty miles north of Vernal—a lone figure sits quietly, cloaked among the dense evergreen and pinyon trees. He remains motionless, simply listening and watching as the setting sun casts gentle rays, creating shadows that stretch westward and dissolve into chaotic, dark lines on the canyon walls. With nothing to do but wait, he is adept at it, knowing how to keep his mind occupied. "Keep it fresh, stay sharp," his mentor used to say, "Focus... focus and then focus some more."

He understands the nature of the game—if it can indeed be called a game—pondering this as he thinks.

Removing his woodland camo baseball cap, he reveals a crop of long, gray infused blonde hair. He wipes the sweat from his brow with the back of his hand. Observing his sweat-streaked hand, he feels the years creeping up on him. "Hell, I'm just a few years north of forty," he thinks, stretching out his legs and scratching the two-day stubble on his face. At just under six feet with a medium build, he considers himself fit as a fiddle, though he acknowledges there's room for improvement. Once a Ranger, always a Ranger, he muses, focusing his piercing blue eyes on the distant stillness. "Hmm," he grunts, lost in thought.

The same question always comes to mind when a kill is imminent: Now the game is on... Focus! As he thinks about the evening's chill—a welcome respite from the afternoon's scorching heat—he slowly raises his thermos cup to his lips and takes a sip. "Damn, this coffee is good," he murmurs, whistling appreciatively.

For a moment, he feels as though he's not here for work at all, but rather relaxing against a tree, soaking in the tranquil sounds of the forest. "This place is great, no, grand—fucking Shangri-La... I love it!" he laughs aloud to himself. As he sits and waits, he contemplates the possibility of moving back to this area, familiar to him from a couple of years spent in Green River and Lima, Wyoming, working as a consultant for major corporations with government contracts after his time in the Army.

Still involved with a company that has facilities in the area, he often visits to fish and pursue other interests. His sparse free time is spent outdoors, hunting and fishing—and not just animals. His training and years as a Ranger, spent in combat and survival in the wilderness, have honed his skills for the long waits and the gritty reality of outdoor life, and the killing, which he has come to relish.

"Well," he playfully croons to the vast emptiness, channeling a spider to its prey, "where are you, my darlings, or something like that." Raising his Steiner Commander binoculars to his eyes, he spots the two climbers. "Ahh... there you are, my little pretties," he laughs playfully.

He has been observing the couple since their first climb that morning at Mustang Ridge, below one of the many overlooks along the North Canyon Rim Red Trail. They weren't hard to find—he knew all about them.

He often muses about the futility of climbing a rock wall, thinking, "A wall... of all things, it doesn't need to be climbed."

"Just a little while longer, folks," he exclaims, taking another sip from his thermos. "Mmm... damn good coffee!"

"I'd better hustle over there to greet you folks, got to get back to my day job," he blurts out as he stands, reaches for his worn brown leather pack with quite a history— not all of it his own—and checks a side pocket to ensure that the crowning jewel of his trip is still there, a reminder of times both good and bad. He has to place it in an inconspicuous spot for everything to work out. Jogging quickly down the North Canyon Ridge Red Trail, he calculates that it will take him about three minutes to cover the distance to Red Rim Canyon Cove, along Mustang Ridge. He aims to arrive with at least six minutes of lead time before the climbers reach the top, hopefully before any other hikers or employees from the nearby Canyon Lodge spot them. As dusk sets in, providing excellent cover, he wonders, "Now, how should I kill them?"

Chapter 8

James Tracy and Rebecca Richmond were on their second climb of the day, having started at 5:00 a.m. for their first climb at Sheep's Creek. Trying to cram in as many climbs as possible each day while they were out here was the rule, not the exception.

Rebecca, long and lean with shoulder-length black hair and dark eyes, stood out with her athletic build and all-American girl smile. She was a freak of nature when it came to rock climbing or any outdoor activity.

James, on the other hand, was her equal in stature and athletic awareness, though a couple of inches taller at 5'11" and about 160 pounds heavier. They complemented each other in many ways.

They planned to average 2-3 small problems over the last three days at Mustang Ridge and the surrounding area, then pack up and catch a flight home to return to the grind by Tuesday.

They were just about to wrap up the day at a little-known red rock location on the Utah side of the reservoir, called Skillet. Some local climbers they had met over the weekend mentioned it to them, describing it as an easy scramble but fun, right below an overlook off the North Canyon Ridge Red Trail.

Although it was about five minutes from a busy lodge area, the climbing location remained largely unpopulated. Skillet had a relatively short approach because of the water and offered various challenges:

slots, cracks, clean holds, and bouldering, unlike the sometimes predictable one-line Sheep's Creek. Skillet also featured a twelve hundred-foot climb with multiple lines back up to the overlook after hiking down. It could be as easy or as difficult as you wanted. For Jim and Reb, as her friends and co-workers called her, free climbing Skillet might not be demanding, but it would definitely be tiring, especially after this morning's session and the recent events in her life affecting her personally. Rebecca's state of mind, tentative at the beginning of the trip, was slowly showing a lack of concern for anything related to climbing.

She was more distracted today, asking Jim to repeat his directions in crucial situations instead of just reacting. She seemed confused. Jim sensed she was struggling with something, and it wasn't her inability to climb.

"The good thing right now," Reb shouted up to Jim, breaking the silence that had enveloped them, "is that I'm glad we don't have to use protection on this slab."

"You know it...quick and easy," replied Jim, who had the lead at the moment. "She's back," he thought. "Good, I'll get her through this." They climbed a few more minutes in silence, enjoying the freedom and expansive beauty. Three times a year, they would leave the confines of the office and go on mini expeditions to get away from corporate America, to purify and self-medicate. God knows it was needed this year.

Jim yelled down to Rebecca, "How are you doing, babe?"

"Fine!" she shot back up to him, jamming a finger hold.

"Hey!...Not much farther," Jim yelled back down to her. Setting up for the next move, in a section that required a heel-toe lock to execute the problem, Jim thought, "Damn, this is the most exciting place to be in the world right now."

For the next 10 minutes, the conversation was minimal as the two climbers concentrated on the climb.

The crux of this climb had finally presented itself, not a moment too soon, as they were exhausted.

Jim shouted down to Reb, who was positioned about 6 feet below him and off to the right, resting.

"Reb, I'm moving up and over to the left. You can walk right in from the position you're in."

"Let's get out of here," he said.

"All right, I am beat," she replied.

The shooter jogged over faster than he anticipated. "This shit really feels good," he thought as he started humming and looking for a comfortable spot to work from.

"Ah!" he voiced as he found what he was looking for, a spot about 10 feet from where he imagined Jim and Rebecca would come out of the canyon.

He sat down, humming more forcefully as the song became stronger in his head, creating an undulating, feverish pitch as his anticipation grew. "Hell, what was the name of that song?...Hmm, oh well!...Time to think about work," he whispered. "Question me this," he spoke in a hushed southern voice, "how should this old boy kill you folks...quickly or slowly?"

"That is something to ponder," he said to himself. "Let's see, slowly I could kill the fella and let him watch me have my way with his girl..."

"She is a damn good-looking little thing...with that ponytail," he said. "Or...I could get freaky and... nah, that's too nasty..."

The shooter thought about how good it would feel to bust the girl up some while she watched her boyfriend die. "Yeah...that would be something...you evil freak..."

But that would leave evidence, and the contract requested a clever and clean kill, just like the other one.

"Well, I guess that means...no sex, damn...and quickly...shit," he replied, answering his earlier question.

"Pity...I could get my perv on!" he remarked.

He started humming again and waited, turning around, reaching into the side pocket of his backpack, and pulling out a Glock 26. He looked at it forlornly before attaching a homemade silencer.

"Man, this beats my nine to five any old day of the week," which reminded him that he needed to make one stop to validate his being out here. "Yes, any old day of the week," he smiled at the thought.

"The Quickness! Yes! Bad Brains, yeah...song rocks," he mumbled, and started humming and waiting.

Chapter 9

Rt 77 South of Cleveland, "Guys, calm down. I fail to see the humor in this situation," Callie commanded as we continued to jab her about the problem and Styles. We had been talking to her on the car's Bluetooth system for a good portion of the trip back home from Pennsylvania.

Ann Callie Banner, at the age of forty-five, was an attractive dark-haired, brown-eyed woman with fine-boned features and a stunning, tall athletic build. She was one hell of a volleyball player in college too.

"Although with Styles' involvement, I can now see where the problem is," she continued. "Now, if one of you would be a sweetheart and talk to Styles about this, we as a firm would appreciate it."

"Yes, Callie, I will handle it," Parker acknowledged.

"Oh! Parker, while you're at it, please call Mr. Schaefer and set up a meet and greet so we can successfully resolve this minor bump in the road."

"Client's wife getting screwed by Styles...nice," Ken smirked, still trying not to laugh again.

"Our reputation is at stake. You guys can't be sleeping around with the clients or their wives," she repeated. "Seriously, that's not the reputation your uncle built this company on."

"Parker, are you stopping by the office on your way home?" Callie asked.

Ken looked at me and shook his head, gesturing "no way."

"No, Callie, it'll be tomorrow morning for both of us if that's okay," he replied.

"Sure, the Mr. Schaefer thing can keep. I will talk to you both in the morning. Enjoy your evening."

"Oh yes! With all of this Mr. Schaefer nonsense, I almost forgot. Parker, we have a meeting in the a.m."

"Yes, new client?" Parker asked.

"Yes, with a friend of yours' sister...name is...Ryan, Mrs. Kelly Ryan," she said.

"Hmm...name doesn't ring a bell...but okay," he said.

"I guess it's a friend of yours from the College of Virginia," she said.

"University, Callie, not college," he corrected.

"Whatever you say, dear. I'll talk to you in the morning," she replied, knowing this would annoy him.

I arrived in Westlake around 6:30 p.m., tired and ready for a hot shower and a drink. Ken and I unloaded the gear and talked for a few minutes in the driveway, and then he was gone. A pile of tangled and dirty climbing gear lay in the middle of the driveway.

"Damn, I'll have to separate and clean the rack gear, which consists of various cams, nuts, and anchors. Also, the ropes will have to be recoiled and cleaned a little better before storing the gear away. Damn him...Ken, you will pay for this in blood," I mumbled, turning to walk towards the garage.

"What, Parker?" I heard a voice coming from the end of my driveway. Startled, I turned quickly in that direction and was greeted by my neighbor John walking his black lab, Julian.

"Oh, you heard me...ah!" I said, quite embarrassed and surprised.

"Yup! Caught that little bit at the end," he said, slowing down to let the dog pee on my lawn. "Kenny screwed you good again, it seems," he laughed.

"Imagine that?" I replied, smiling. "How's the family?" I asked.

"They are good. I'm good. Thanks for asking."

"You look good, Parker. No new bruises or bullet holes that I can see," he replied, smiling.

"Ah...yeah, thanks for your loving and caring concern, John," I grinned.

"Well, it's just my neighborly observation and concern for your well-being," he remarked. "Have a nice evening, Parker. Julian, come on boy, let's go!"

"Yep, later John."

Chapter 10

Leaving the pile in the driveway, I tapped in my security code and waited for the garage to open. Bark, my 100-pound collie, charged at me like a runaway freight train, tongue hanging out and tail wagging with happiness. I gave him a big hug and rubbed his head, and he returned the affection with a wet doggie kiss.

"What's up, Big Daddy Mac? You big old guy, you," I said, bending down joyfully to rub his chest and pat his head.

After a few more licks and head butts, I stood up and surveyed the kitchen, remembering the pile in the driveway. "You can go out with me to clean up after I get a drink!" I said to the panting machine.

Opening the fridge and grabbing two bottles of water, I twisted the cap off one and stood there mulling over the completion of my finished kitchen. A new Wolf stove, a Bosch dishwasher, and a Sub-Zero refrigerator were installed into the surrounding huge Robenet cabinetry. I still needed to get some furniture for the dining room and the other bedrooms.

The contractor, a friend of Callie's, installed all the new cabinets and built a center island that houses the sink and a wine refrigerator. All of the countertops were finished with granite—a nice touch, I thought, marveling. "Loving it!" I said to Bark and finished off the bottle of water.

Walking over to Bark's dish, I poured the other bottle of water.

It took me about an hour and a half to clean and coil the ropes and miscellaneous gear, all the while thinking of how to get back at Ken. After putting my gear away and stuffing Ken's into the trunk of my car, I took Bark for a quick walk down to the wooded area behind my house.

My house is located on the far northwestern edge of Westlake, a good-sized suburb of about 33,000 people, roughly 16 miles west of downtown Cleveland. It's a special mix of open space and show-stopping trees, so I'm told, and a pretty nice place to raise a family.

I bought the house here three years ago at Callie's urging. A couple of her friends were going through a nasty divorce, and the house was 95% finished. So, I got the house at an unreal price and took it off their hands; neither one wanted the other to have it.

It's a modern colonial, 2,900 sq. ft. with an open floor plan, vaulted ceilings, 2 1/2 bathrooms, 4 bedrooms, an office, and a fully finished basement. There's a 2 1/2 car garage built on 2 acres located on a dead-end street of a new development. Behind the houses on this side of the street are undeveloped woods that run about 1/8 mile before you see the next development and Ohio State Route 90 to the north.

"Yeah, pretty nice," I said to myself, thinking about the location.

Bark and I returned from our walk, and it was time for me to get a shower and mellow out for the evening. I was on my way upstairs when I noticed the lights blinking on the answering machine. Ignoring the phone for the moment, I went to clean up.

Dressed in cargo shorts and an old Santa Cruz skateboard t-shirt, I poured myself a glass of Woodford Reserve Double Oak. Opening the screen door, I called Bark in for dinner. He was over by the left corner of the yard and seemed to be paying a great deal of attention to something in the woods.

"Skunk," I thought. "Bark, come on boy… Bark, Bark, get over here, big guy."

It was just starting to get dark, and the evening sky was a melting yellow/orange, meandering into a purple star-filled blanket.

"What do you see out there, big guy?" I said, bending down to rub his head. "Okay, let's see who wants to make old Parker happy today," I said, pushing play on the answering machine.

There was a message from Erin, my ex-girlfriend of two years, who had recently dumped me.

I took a tall pull from my glass of bourbon. "Aha... yes, that hit the old spot," I said aloud.

My thoughts drifted to the dark sweetness and rugged taste of bourbon as her voice droned on about how bad she felt and that it was in the best interest of both of us to go our separate ways. Really?

"Get a life! Wait, you now have one, silly me," I said, responding to her babbling.

I hit next a couple more times. Friends and the UVA alumni office made up the bulk of the remaining messages—nothing too interesting. The phone rang just as I was in the middle of pouring a drink. Thinking it might be Ken, I decided to let the machine screen it. Not Ken!

There was a long pause, then a familiar voice that I hadn't heard in a long time and didn't expect to hear from either.

Chapter 11

Sitting not more than a mile away in his car, Holtz Kovach watched the Friday night crowd walk in and out of the Cinnamon Delta Blues Club, located in a popular plaza on Detroit Road across from Crocker Park. The rhythm of the music wafting through the constant opening and closing of the club door caused Holtz to tap out a syncopated beat on his chin with his cell phone. The message he had just left was perfect. He had big plans for Parker and company.

"Yeah, good. I'm in your head. Ooh! Got a flight to catch!" he said icily, looking at his watch. Throwing the prepaid phone onto the passenger seat, he started the car, pulled out of the parking lot, turned left onto Detroit Road, and accelerated towards Rt 90 East and the airport. He smiled, replaying the message he had just left on Parker's voicemail in his head.

"Parker, how are you? (pause) I know you're not there, out with Ken... yes! Am I not right? Ah. On another climbing or fun biking adventure, hmm? I know you feel that I am responsible for Jim's death somehow. Maybe I am... maybe I'm not! (pause) Interesting... though, if you really want to place the blame on someone, I guess I would fit the criteria. Kind of convenient, wouldn't you say? Yes! Oh, and before I go, for now... please give Ann my best. She'll know what I mean."

The message ended abruptly. I played it again, not believing that the asshole would call me. It was the voice of someone I truly hated and would kill if given the opportunity. Thinking back and knowing that this piece of crap was the last person to see Big Jim alive— and he lied about it time and time again—now he was calling me. I felt truly evil and out of control.

"Mellow... get control of yourself, Parker... relax... relax... mellow," I said to myself.

I walked over, poured myself another stiff drink, and called the two people who could help me sort this out rationally and under the radar of all others. Picking up the phone, I dialed a 216 prefix. The call was answered after two rings.

"What took you so long, little brother?" said the voice on the other end, in a strong tenor.

"Damn! Ant, I love you too, and I got your message earlier today, bro," I replied.

"Yeah, you know me—impatient to the point of obnoxious... besides, not doing much," Ant said.

"Cool. Hey, thanks, I appreciate you getting back quickly with the text and voice message," I said.

"Ah, okay! How's Callie and the business doing?" he asked, laughing smoothly.

"Callie? Shit, Ant, she's tough as the Rock of Gibraltar," I said. "And as for the business, it's booming! Keeps me working hard. Got a couple of cases that Callie is shifting your way."

"Cool! We'll see what we can do for you. You know the lady is good, and you're okay when you're not getting people killed," Ant chuckled.

"Me? What... Dude, I am an upstanding guy!" I joked back at him.

"Yeah, yeah, and the pope is black. Wait a sec, let me put the guy on, Parker."

Ant and the Ghost are investigators for a very large law firm that shall remain anonymous, and they do freelance projects on the side for a select few anonymous clients such as MRO. It helps to be friends. Ant and Ghost can get to places where I have no resources, like a lot of the inner-city areas, with their street sources. So we trade off a lot of cases and help each other out with each other's resources. Besides, Ghost is a distant cousin of mine. I have a lot of family on both sides of the proverbial fence.

"Okay, P, I'm transferring your call... later, bro," he said.

"Parker, Parker... little bro, how are you this fine Friday evening?" a deep southern baritone, smooth as butter, questioned me warmly.

"A tad bit troubled, Ghost

"Ghost!... Umm... I got a call from someone from the past," I said quietly, walking to the large window that looked out into the front yard from the family room.

"This, by chance, would be the same someone allegedly associated with Big Jim's disappearance, I presume."

"You guessed correctly," I said to Ghost.

"Please do tell, little bro. Enlighten me. I have a feeling this may get nasty if it's who I think it is," he laughed. I proceeded to explain the cryptic phone message, and he explained his reason for wanting to talk to me. Picking up the remote, I turned the stereo on, and the sweet sounds of Brooke Fraser's voice filled the room. It felt good to laugh for the moment because Ghost was right—shit was going to get ugly when it came to Holtz Kovach.

"So, you think the crazy motherfucker did Big J?" he questioned, answering his own thought.

"Yes!... He all but suggested that in the voice message, damn near confessing... I have a gut feeling about this one."

"Trust me... there are a lot of coincidental things happening with the case," I pointed out, frustrated.

"I believe you," he said.

"A lot of what was going on with the investigation did not seem like it pointed to an accident."

"I believe that Ranger Whip Jordan knew that as well," Ghost surmised.

Whip Jordan is the ranger in Ashley National Forest who found key evidence in Big Jim's disappearance.

"By the way, have you heard from him?"

"Not for a couple of weeks, and everything he explained to me, I passed on to you," I said.

"Although it could be the sheriff's department and their skepticism."

"I don't know! Copy that voice message and send it to Kroy for safekeeping," he suggested.

Kroy Burroughs is legal counsel for MRO and a close friend of the family.

"Yeah... I'll get it done."

"Tell you what, P, are you working on anything hot at the moment?" Ghost asked.

"No, just finished the Schaefer case, and Callie has me meeting someone in the morning. No idea what it's about," I said, looking over at what the dog was doing.

"I am sure it can be assigned to Little or Rasur if it pans out to be a domestic or a white-collar case."

Little John Raynaks and Rasur Gutierrez are seasoned, long-time private investigators for MRO and handle the bulk of general cases. Little, as he is called by everyone, is a weapons and surveillance expert, and Rasur, whom I call Potsee, is a computer and surveillance expert. Both men are irreplaceable at MRO.

"Ok then, let me finish up some things here that I am currently involved in, and I'll help where needed if that's cool with you."

"Sounds good, Ghost. I'll shake something loose up that way and see what blows back," I responded.

"P, watch your ass. It sounds like Holtz is up to something, and he might be around here. Let Callie know too," he warned.

"Shit, Ghost, I really don't want to go there... but yeah, you're right, she's got to know about the call."

"P! Shit is more than likely going to get really nasty. The guy is good... you up for that, bro?"

"Yeah, I understand... it's part of the plan," I said with dread in my voice.

"Cool, just seeing where your head is... Oh, by the way, I have a gift for the little man," he said.

"It's a Daly ZDA 9mm that he's been asking about."

"Tell him the damn little thing is a creepy little gun. It's got a trigger on it like an AK-47."

"I'm sure Little John will love it, and I'll relay the message in the morning," I said, laughing.

"Ok, I'll talk to you later in the week, bro," he signed off, laughing about the idiosyncrasies of the gun.

"See ya..." I said, still grinning.

Chapter 12

7:00 a.m. came quickly and harshly, with the painful sing-song and chirpy chatter of birds performing a joyful concerto. Mix this with the unmistakable sounds of Captain and Tennille crooning one of their hits on my alarm clock radio. "Oh... God!" I murmured. "Love... Love will keep us together..." they sang as I lay there, beaten from exhaustion and too many single malts last night.

"Shit it will..." I replied to the song's lyrics, rolling over to take my first peek at the morning sun filtering through the slightly parted blinds in my bedroom.

Giving in to the less-than-favorable intrusion of this song, I sat up in bed. Rubbing a hand over my face and through my hair, I quickly surveyed my surroundings, gathered my thoughts, and decided to lie back down. There, I had now confronted the morning demons and made a conscious decision to sleep for a few more minutes. Closing my eyes, I could still see and feel the early morning brightness, not to mention hear it too. Looking up at the ceiling fan, eyes wide open, I thought about what the day held in store for me. Work and more work. I figured I might as well get my lazy ass up, still I mused...

After what seemed like a good five minutes of reflecting, but was really only about one minute, I jumped out of bed and into the adjoining bathroom, disconsolate about getting up. The music selection was not helping my motivation either.

A quick and revitalizing shower provided me with a much-needed burst of energy.

Chancing a look in the mirror, I was profoundly reminded that a shave was needed, and needed it was.

Grabbing my robe and venturing downstairs, I found Bark lazily lying by the Rear door, waiting to go out. Patting him on his head, I looked over and noticed that the answering machine light was blinking.

"Hmm! Someone must have called late last night or early this morning?"

"Mmm, don't remember the phone ringing," I said to Bark as I let him out.

I must have slept like the dead. Heck, I was really tired after yesterday's climbing session, thinking back.

"Ok, Parker, first things first. Let's get this party started," I thought, looking out into the backyard as the dog was on his way back to the house, content and happy. "Coffee!" I said and let Bark back into the house as he looked at me with silent understanding.

I fed Bark and left him alone to devour his feast. Sitting down in the kitchen, I sipped my first of perhaps many cups of coffee to come this morning. It was time to focus on what was to happen today and what was not going to happen. "No riding today," I mumbled, eliminating that plan.

"Right... no fun today, just work," I verbalized out loud in a croaking voice.

Wrong! I thought as a sly, wicked smile worked its way across my freshly shaven face.

"Damn! I forgot!" I poured myself another cup of coffee, grabbed the paper, and walked over to the answering machine, staring at it. Sitting down on a stool at the counter, I imagined that this call was from the office canceling the meet and greet.

Now that would be a real convenience, and then back to bed would be a reality. I pushed play.

The voice that bellowed from my answering machine was so irritating and riled that it deeply disturbed the tranquility and peacefulness of the morning. Except there were still the birds... and work. Ugh! God, Big Al Schaefer had caught up with me, and at home no less! This was not a good sign as to how my day might shake out. Crap, Al was raving about how wrong my agency was and that he had paid good money for bad answers to his problem and that he would have the last laugh.

"Whew... right, tell me something new!" I moaned and erased the message.

There was a second message, and it was a little more interesting: it was the voice of a woman and quite stressed, it seemed.

"...Parker McIntyre... Mr. McIntyre, (pause) this is Kelly Ryan. If you receive this message this evening..."

The message was not finished, and the call went dead with just a dial tone.

Hmm, now this I considered interesting, if not confusing.

How are all these people getting my private home line?

Playing back the message again, I was rewarded with the same cryptic and perplexing partial dispatch.

Chapter 13

The woman said her name was Kelly Ryan. The name sounded familiar, though I guessed she wasn't a long-forgotten girlfriend. Sitting there, thinking and sipping my now-warm cup of coffee, which I usually like piping hot, I tried to refocus on where I had heard the name before. Uneasiness clouded my thoughts, but I had no success.

"Huh!" I grunted as I walked over to the microwave to reheat my coffee. My meet-and-greet this morning was with someone named Ryan... Kelly! Yeah.

"Damn, that didn't take long to figure out, Sherlock," I shouted, grabbing my coffee and heading upstairs.

Throwing on some jeans, a University of Virginia Lacrosse t-shirt, and my favorite Salomon running shoes, I looked for my favorite gift from Uncle Cyrus—a sweet Timex chronograph. It wasn't where I normally put it. "Damn, where's that watch?" I said. Dressed and feeling awake but not well, I went into my office to get a weapon, something I didn't always carry. With Holtz running around again, it wouldn't hurt to start now.

"Son of a bitch!" I mumbled out loud, stepping on the watch as I walked around the desk.

Little John said to bring one of the Sigs down to the office next time I was in. He suggested the Dak since it's the one I use the most out of the four handguns I own, which include a SIG P229 RS, a Kahr PM9, and a

Springfield Arms .45. He was going to add some high-tech modifications to the piece.

Opening the wall safe in the closet, I removed a SIG Sauer P229 Dak and its carrying holster, given to me by Uncle Jim upon completion of my investigator's license. It gets the job done, you know!

Patting Bark on the head, I grabbed my attaché case, a new high-tech titanium thing with a digital combo lock. I always keep it open on the desk and put the Dak in a specially designed pocket used for carrying larger items.

Picking up the attaché, I proceeded towards the garage, wondering if I had forgotten something.

Stopping in the kitchen, I grabbed a donut out of the box on the counter—guilty pleasures—and headed out.

"Damn it!" I said, stopping the car before the end of the driveway and running back into the house.

I had forgotten my iPhone. Retrieving it from the kitchen counter, I walked over to the dishwasher, grabbed a thermos, and poured the remnants of the coffee into it. Grabbing the box of donuts, I left again. Bark was lying by the rear door and raised his head to look at me in passing.

"Shut up, don't bark a word. I forgot coffee," I said and walked out. Back in the car, I armed the alarm from my cell phone, took a swig of coffee, and headed down to Bradley Rd and onto Detroit Ave, and the big world this Saturday morning.

The traffic was considerably light as I headed east towards Cahoon Ave and the offices of McIntyre Reed & O'Brien.

Relaxed and feeling good by my standards, I put in a new CD: The Life and Times, a cool indie band from the Midwest or somewhere flat in the geography of the U.S.

"Fools in love... it isn't what it seems... Fools in love... The thrill of victory." The singer crooned to a smooth rock-oriented groove. I bobbed my head in time and surmised about it. You've got to be a fool to fall in love, basing my ideology on my own failed relationships. I was hoping to clear my head before arriving at the zoo, our nickname for MRO.

Finding out why Kelly Ryan needed to call me at home knifed through my grooving brain so sharply it felt like someone was sitting in the car beside me, poking me in the head.

The abrupt disconnection and the hurried tone in her voice—or was it panic? This will be interesting to find out... I hope.

Looking ahead, Cahoon Ave was slowly approaching, and so was my turn-off to the zoo.

Chapter 14

8:45 a.m. - MRO's parking lot looked quite busy, with five cars and a delivery truck.

I pulled in and checked my Rearview mirror as I parked between a dark brown Volvo SUV and a dark grey Audi A4.

Looking over to my left, I saw Styles' tricked-out Honda Civic instead of the tricked-out cafe racer that he rode fast a lot. Great! Looks like I will have to intervene between him and Callie, I imagined, climbing out of the car. This is something I do a lot around the office; maybe I should have become a psychologist or a mediator. Three of the other vehicles here I recognized; the other two, I had no idea.

I wondered if the client was here for our meet-and-greet.

Opening the front door, I was greeted by the sweet aroma of some exotic coffee blend and the music of Ryuichi Sakamoto.

The offices of McIntyre, Reed, and O'Brien are housed in a good-sized warehouse measuring about 120,000 sq. feet, located in a mixed business district off Cahoon Rd near I-90 in Westlake, just before Bay Village. Westlake, the city where our office is located, is also where I reside. It's nestled between Bay Village to the north, Avon to the west, and North Olmsted to the south.

The sprawling metropolis of Cleveland is about 16.2 miles east of these fast-growing and affluent suburbs. The distance, in fact, does not separate the suburbs from the realities of crime in the big city.

MRO, as we are known by clients and local law enforcement officials, is a high-profile and respected investigation firm that cooperates and works well within the parameters set by the law enforcement community. Big Jim McIntyre took great care in establishing this precedence back when the agency first started. The McIntyre family has owned the real estate that the warehouse sits on for years, which helps out greatly. The offices are laid out on two floors; on the ground level, you have a reception area where Callie and the clients sit.

There are two offices on this floor, a smaller conference room, and a kitchen. Behind the first-floor conference room is the remaining warehouse space, which has a firing range, a skateboarding half-pipe, and a climbing wall. Various sporting items are either hung or stored in organized bins and shelves throughout the opposite side of the firing range area. On the second level, there are three more offices and a larger conference room. It is here, in the upstairs or main room, that all of the strategy sessions are worked on with various parties involved in a particular case.

To get to the upper floor, you have two staircases: one in the front, set between Callie's desk and the entrance to the ground-level offices, and one in the rear leading up from the firing range. The upper level has a 3-foot wall/railing surrounding the platform that it's built on, giving it an open floor plan.

So, you can be in the conference room or any one of the offices and look down at people or at the firing range. Callie was at her desk, on the phone, looking at her computer screen when I walked in.

She looked up and pointed towards the stairs, while mouthing the words, "She's upstairs."

I smiled and blew her a kiss. God, I love that woman.

"Family!" I said to myself, reminding myself of how good it feels to have them.

"Call Chase, make a mental note of this," I said as I climbed the stairs two at a time.

Upon reaching the top of the stairs, I heard Styles and Rasur talking about last night's conquest—young women at the newest Cleveland hot spot on West 6th, the Power Factory upstairs and the Play House downstairs.

I looked into Little John's office as Styles described some woman named Jules and her gladdening fondness for the reverse cowgirl sexual position. Styles, a former defensive back in college, is six feet two and a muscled two hundred and twenty pounds of woman-crazed playboy. He stopped mid-thought as I walked in, smiling. "What's up, P-Mac?" he said, reaching over to give me some knuckles.

Reciprocating the knuckle handshake, it's a guy thing, I replied, "You, man. How's it going?"

"Like always, I'm in the zone, charged and waiting for the next case," Styles said.

"Down boy, get a grip," I signaled with my hand.

Rasur reached over during this exchange and slapped my hand, "Howdy." Rasur is a bespectacled, curly-haired, dark-complected, elfish-looking thirty-five-year-old genius. He said dryly, "Howdy hi back at you."

"Cool now. Hey! Did anyone talk to Callie yet?" I asked, looking at Styles. "No," he replied.

"Well, here's a thought: if you are screwing Al's wife Misty, don't let it happen! Please."

"Don't want to hear... not one filthy... bit!" I said. "Callie's not too happy either, not to mention Al."

"How mad is she?" he asked. "Lukewarm to boiling mad. It depends," I said. "Don't push it!"

"Also, I will take the heat from Al for you. Oh yes, and thanks for the help on the case," I mentioned.

"No problem," Styles said. "Now how about some pay? And oh yeah..."

"My boss and your lawyer want to know if you can give him a call sometime soon."

"Tell your uncle I will do that," I said.

"Hey Parker," Rasur said. "There is a young lady waiting to see you in the conference room."

"A volleyball player," Styles said quickly. "I don't know, tennis," Rasur objected.

"Athlete!" Styles replied. "What's the deal?" I said.

"You'll see," Rasur smiled and growled. "Where is Little John?" I asked both of them.

"He's downstairs, drooling over the gift that Ghost sent him," Styles said.

Rasur picked up where Styles left off, "A Charles Daly ZDA 9mm, and he's field-stripping it right now."

"Nice," I said. "Well, let me go and see our company."

"She's early. I'll talk to you guys later. Go Cavaliers!" I yelled at both of them. They are Hurricanes fans.

"Hmm! Nothing said, they are a weak team this year!" I thought, moving on.

Chapter 15

"She's going into a private investigation service," the man whispered, the toothpick annoyingly bobbing with every syllable. They had followed the attractive brunette from her condo, where they had been sent to keep tabs on her that morning.

Not a bad assignment so far. "Private Detective..." He took a last drag off the cigarette, sucking in the cancer and exhaling its remnants out the partially open window.

"What'd be the diff, man?" Slim retorted.

"Not a problem! Slick... I mean Slim, I better call you-know-who."

Carl "Bang" Smitts and Slim Jenkins were associates of Marcella Lopez, a local businessman with his hands firmly entrenched in the import-export business, which pretty much means drugs, arms, and all sorts of underhanded activities. He's one of those guys that the authorities have a hard time prosecuting—one slick and mean dude. It is a known fact that he has killed people, but again, no body, no crime. Marcella grew up in the tough Cherry Hill area of Baltimore, migrating to Cleveland as a former college basketball player.

"She's at MRO, that private investigation service out here in Westlake," Bang blew into the phone. Slim reached into a cigarette case, pulled out a joint, held it up to his partner, smiling and mouthing the words, "You good?" Bang was listening to the voice on the cell and nodded, using his other hand to give the thumbs-up salute for okay. "...I understand... so just leave the tail on and watch..." He responded, trailing off, "Ok, got it. We will wait, but this shit is getting boring."

"Yeah, I agree... need some action... okay, you're the boss." He disconnected.

Taking a deep hit from the joint, Slim held the smoke in, releasing it and smiling. "Now that's the shit, man," he coughed, passing it. "Soooo, what's the haps?" he asked. Holding his hand up and following suit, simulating Slim, Bang repeated the process and after a prolonged coughing fit, said they were to sit on her and look for the opportunity to grab her. "Hot! Gotta turn the air on, man." Slim agreed, "Gotta be one of the hottest Augusts in a long time." Bang nodded and took another puff.

Chapter 16

I stopped in the doorway of Conference Room A and knocked so that I wouldn't startle our guest. She turned around, smiling, and said, "Thanks, but I heard you guys down the hall."

"So, I knew you were here."

I just stood there smiling.

"And oh, swimming is the answer," she said.

I laughed and said, "Alright then."

I held out my hand and said, "I'm Parker McIntyre, pleased to make your acquaintance."

She took my hand in an assured grip, her soft hands conveying confidence. "Likewise, I am Kelly Ryan."

"We have a 9:10 meeting this morning. I'm early."

"Yes," I replied. "I called yesterday and talked to Callie Banner."

"Yes, she informed me," I said.

I must've looked like a fool because I just kept staring at her.

"Is there something wrong?" she asked.

"Oh no, I'm just trying to put things into perspective," I said.

She was—or should I say is—remarkably attractive, 5'8" with an athletic build and green eyes that played off her brown hair. "Interesting," I mused.

Shaking my head and shrugging my shoulders, I turned and sat down.

"Okay… Can I get you something to drink?" I asked.

"Nothing right now, thank you," she replied.

"You know, you're nothing like I expected."

"Oh!" I said, quite amused and confused.

"No, what I mean is, my expectations were… hmm, how shall I put this?" she said with a searching look. "The name! I thought you were Irish… well, I mean you can still be Irish…"

"Never mind… I don't really know what I mean, I'm just babbling... this is upsetting," she resigned.

I sat there smiling, knowing that she was growing uncomfortable by the minute.

Finally, I figured I'd better throw a life preserver. I held up my hands and said, "It's the Black Factor."

She looked at me, confused. "The what?" she said.

"The Black Factor," I said. "It's something that I have learned to live with for years and will continue to live with." I smirked.

She still looked confused.

"I mean, I have an Irish last name and an English first name. People automatically assume that I am white. Sorry about that."

"…Will this be a problem?" I asked her with a smile.

Kelly started laughing hysterically and squeezed out a "no…"

"No! Absolutely not," she responded, still laughing.

"Good!" I said.

"But I've never heard of the Black Factor," she laughed.

"It's just something that I made up."

"I hope that I didn't insult you, Parker," Kelly inferred after regaining her composure.

"No, you certainly did not," I said.

"Well, just to clear the air, I am half Irish on my father's side and half African American on my mother's side. Just for the record."

"Well, that's cool, honestly, Parker. You don't have to explain," she said, uncomfortable.

"Well then, with that settled, let's move forward," I beamed.

Strangely, we looked at each other and started laughing again. It felt good for a minute or so.

This was good because I could sense that the dread was about to come, and soon was now.

"Whew, all right, whew... okay," I said, attempting to serious up the situation. "Well, Kelly, what brings you here on a nice Saturday?" I asked.

The vibe over the last few minutes seemed to evaporate with that question.

Leave it to old Parker to mess up a good time, I thought as Kelly's smile was replaced with a frown.

"Well, it's about my brother," she said. "He's dead! Murdered!" she said pointedly.

"You knew my brother, Guy!"

I must've had a puzzled look on my face because she repeated his name with a little more emphasis and concern. "Guy Ryan... University of Virginia? Your frat brother!"

I said nothing, just sat there thinking, and then it hit me with the force of a George Foreman blow to my head.

I blurted out in an unsure voice, "Robbie?"

She responded by nodding her head and pursing her lips as if to keep from breaking down and crying.

"You mean Robbie Ryan is your brother?" I questioned.

"Yes, we call him Guy. It's his middle name," Kelly said.

"I'm sorry it didn't register right away," I said. "How... It's been quite a while since I last saw him."

"Shit!" I said again.

"Yes... He's dead! Murdered two days ago," she said.

"Umm... okay," I said and took a deep breath.

Still at a loss for words as this horrific situation played over in my mind, I wondered how I had no clue until now. "You didn't know about it, Parker?" she asked questionably.

"Not a damn clue, I don't think…" I said. "Please… I am sorry for you and your family's loss."

"This is quite a shock," I responded.

"Yes, it is," she said.

"Bill, our oldest brother, is taking it quite hard. He and Guy were really close. That's not to say that I am not upset either," she continued. "Now it's only Bill and me left."

"Mom and Dad have been gone for a few years now," she explained. "Now Guy, in this senseless manner."

"Yes," I said and nodded as I listened to her, not really knowing what to say.

"Please tell me about what happened and why you think it's murder."

Chapter 17

"Well, he was shot in cold blood along with another person, a girl."

"This took place on June 1st at West Branch State Park in Ravenna." She paused to reflect.

"Shit... hold on, Kelly. I heard about this crime," I said.

"I had no idea it was Robbie... err, Guy."

"I do not know much about the particulars... sorry to interrupt you, please continue," I said.

"Well, they were both shot at point-blank range in the face and left to die in the woods."

"That's basically all that I know. It's still an open investigation, and the sheriff's department and the state police are playing it, as they said, close to the vest." She took a deep breath and then exhaled.

Again, I sat there silently, contemplating what she was explaining to me, wondering how this got by me.

No one from the fraternity has called about this or seemed to care.

I was still sitting there, staring, thinking about my own inability to stay in contact with friends and family and how this one got by.

"Parker, now I could use something to drink, please, if you don't mind," she said.

"Absolutely... I was just wondering why no one contacted me before your visit today," I said, getting up. "What would you like? Coffee, water, tea, or a pop?" I asked.

"How about something stronger? I sure as hell could use it right now," she responded.

"Ok! How about some..." She cut me off, saying that water would do just fine.

I went to the refrigerator and retrieved a couple of bottles of Perrier, which seemed to be the flavor of the month. "Would you like a glass?" I asked.

"No thanks, I'm good," she said, crossing and then uncrossing her shapely long legs.

Taking a sip of water, she then took a deep breath and said, "Ok, I'm cool. Where was I?"

"Oh yes, as I said, two days ago at West Branch State Park, and they have no witnesses."

"Yes, I know the place; I've been there before," I said.

"So, it's the park police and the sheriff's department handling the investigation!"

"And not the state police, right?"

I put this as a question and a statement, hoping she could confirm my belief that if the state police were handling this investigation, I would not get a shred of information from them. They don't like me.

"Yes, it's both the park police and the sheriff's department handling the investigation. They are sharing it," Kelly said. "Oh, I'm sorry, Parker. I meant park police earlier; I incorrectly said state police. I apologize."

"The case is still an open investigation, and they still don't have any suspects."

"Nothing! Not a damn thing in the way of evidence, at least that's what they're telling me," she said.

"Have they told you anything about the direction in which the investigation is going?" I asked.

"No, nothing! Outside the basic generic condolences and that they are working on it."

"Or that they are still hoping to find someone who saw something and will decide to come forward with information."

"Ok, I see," I said.

Chapter 18

"Kelly, with the sheriff's department and the park police handling the investigation, I don't know how I could help you," I replied, thinking hard about this.

"Well, I had hoped that because you knew my brother, you would look into this as a favor. Besides, I know what the investigating authorities are saying... and it's not true!"

"I see. Kelly, let me ask you this out of curiosity: how did you hear about me or MRO for that matter?" I asked.

"Guy left me explicit instructions that mentioned contacting you if something happened to him. It was almost like he knew his death was imminent," she said.

"Hmm, that's an interesting bit of info," I said. "Did Guy have anyone or anything to fear?"

"Not to my knowledge," she inferred.

"How did he inform you to contact me?" I asked, wondering how odd this whole situation was.

"Well, let me see. Actually, it was twice that he mentioned you. The first time, we were out at The Brewing Co, and he started talking about his job. He wanted to talk about something at his job that disturbed him, but that never happened," she said.

"Why not?" I asked.

"Well, instead he started talking about UVa and some of the good old times and how he really did..." She paused for a few seconds to gather herself. "Excuse me... need to stay in contact with some of his bros, especially Parker," she said.

"I thought, okay, what's the hidden agenda for all the self-disclosure? I sincerely hoped that he was alright and dismissed his actions to the drinks we were having," she expressed. "Then out of the blue, he now wants to talk about my new project at work... it was..." She trailed off, as if in thought, searching for the right words. "...was...was... very strange!" she said.

"We never talk about work—that's a rule we established early on for our R&R nights out. I really don't know what was on his mind that night. He was all over the place!" she said, quite exasperated.

"Really? Do you think it was stress from the job?" I remarked.

"I have no answer. He was going through changes in his personal life, a new girl he was crazy about. Actually, she was the other person killed that day—Laurie Rice. She was a co-worker of his at Systech Technologies in Ravenna."

Chapter 19

"Hmm," I said. "You mentioned that Robbie brought me up twice. Was it the night you both went out for the last time?" I asked.

"No, let me correct that. I mean, he mentioned you verbally..." She paused. "And then! Your name came up again later. Let me explain," she said.

"A letter arrived, care of Guy Ryan, sent to my home with no return address. I was going to give it to him the next time I saw him, but we know that didn't happen. After Guy's death, I decided to open the letter," she said.

"What were the contents of the letter?" I asked.

"The question is not what the contents are, but where they are... weird!" she exclaimed.

"How so?" I asked, quite curious.

Sitting up and leaning forward in the chair, she put her hands, fingertips forward, on her thighs and said, "Well, three things. First, the envelope contained some pictures of Guy, Laurie, and two other people hiking. There was a group shot and then a couple's shot, somewhere in one of the big mountain states. And a piece of paper that someone started to type a note on but did not finish," she said.

I listened, intrigued. "It said, 'Give these items to...' That was it. But secondly, on the back of one of the pictures, it said, 'P. McIntyre and USB... eerie.'"

After she said this, I sat thinking about the hard, consequential nature of having my name on a picture associated with the murder of two people—one that I knew and the other three that I had no idea about.

Kelly asked, "Are you okay?"

I must have had a confused look on my face because, well, I simply was. "Oh yeah... yes, just processing what you said. Hmm, interesting, to say the least."

"Process this: there wasn't a USB drive in the envelope." She gestured with open palms out. "If there was supposed to be... I didn't see any!" Kelly continued.

After Kelly had explained all of this last development to me, I sat listening intently, trying to make sense of the circumstances surrounding the death of her brother and his girlfriend.

I snapped back as Kelly asked me if I thought the following development was not odd.

"Yes, indeed, this is strange," I said. "Kelly, did you inform the authorities about this suspicious package you received?"

"No, I didn't think much about it in the beginning. My mind was in scatterbrain mode."

"Understandable... okay, you said there were three things," I said.

"It wasn't until I saw that another employee of Systech was killed that I got concerned."

This little announcement caught me off guard and sure as hell intrigued my interest. "What other employee's death?" I asked.

"Two, actually," she said.

"What are their names?" I asked.

"I believe their names are Rebecca Richmond and James Tracy."

"Interesting... do you think the two in the picture might be them?" I asked.

She shrugged her shoulders and bit her lip, nodding her head slowly.

"Kelly," I said, blowing out a quick breath of air and rubbing my forehead, "at some point you will have to turn that envelope over to the sheriff's department. It's evidence."

"But... hold on to it until I talk to someone in the sheriff's office. In the meantime, I will look around and see what's what... and if I can find out anything. I can't guarantee you anything will come from this, but we will see," I said. "With my name on those pictures, that might be our in to getting some info." I wondered what I had gotten into.

"Good then! Parker, really, thanks a lot for looking into this craziness. I am sure Guy would..." She started to choke up in an emotional moment, thinking of her brother in the past tense. "...appreciate it, and so do I. Thank you again," she said.

"No problem. It's the least I could do," I said. "What is your normal fee for investigating?"

"Don't worry about that right now. I'm not sure what we have yet."

"Where can I reach you if I find something?" I asked her.

She reached into her purse and pulled out a business card and a pen. "Here's my card, and I'll write my cell and home number on it for you. Feel free to contact me anytime."

I took the business card from her and held it up to read it. I recognized the company insignia embossed on the card. "Bennett, Sweitzer, and Johnson. You're an architect?"

"Yes," she replied.

"I've heard of you folks," I smiled. "That's some impressive work your firm did on that living space over in Ohio City," I complimented.

"Thank you. It was one of the first projects that they let me sink my teeth into when I came on board," she beamed.

"Cool," I replied.

We were both distracted by someone singing in the hallway, walking in our direction. Turning around to look towards the door, we were both greeted by Ken and Little John poking their heads into the conference room, and they smiled.

Chapter 20

"Good morning, P-Mac... and whoa! Wait a minute. Hello there. My name is Ken..."

"Ken Roberts, at your service, little lady," he said with a wide smile.

"Down, boy!" I said, gesturing for him to come into the office.

Without hesitation, he stepped into the room with his hand outstretched, making a beeline directly toward Kelly as if no one else was in the immediate area.

Kelly stood up, took Ken's outstretched hand, shook it firmly, and introduced herself. Turning around, she did the same with Little John, who had followed a somewhat overbearing Ken into the room.

With the introductions finished, I turned to sit down and continue the meeting when Little John said, "Please excuse me, Ms. Ryan, but I need a word with Parker if you don't mind."

Standing six feet four, John Rasuk is anything but little—a boyish-looking man with small round glasses and a shock of unruly brown-blonde hair upon his head. "This won't take but a moment," he said.

"That's okay, Mr. Little John, we were about to finish up," she said, smiling. "Please call me John," he said.

"Okay, John. Call me Kelly," she replied, staring up at him.

"Okay, now... PARKER! I need to know where your gun is. I am leaving here in about an hour, and as I told you Thursday, I have that laser sight to retrofit on it, and your new X300 tactical light is here. So where is it, and did you bring the right weapon?" Little John asked in his no-nonsense manner.

"Yes and yes. It's in the office, on the floor next to my attaché case," I replied.

"That's a nice place, PARKER!" he said, quite surprised and emphasizing my name again. "I'm afraid I need to get on with this, so I must bid you all a good day. It was especially nice to meet you, Kelly." Little John walked quickly towards the door, stopping abruptly and turning around. He looked directly at me and said, "I know this might be difficult for you to comprehend, but please test fire your weapon today, okay?"

"Oh, and yeah, your Garrett Nash holster is here in the conference room. Please, please, Parker, test fire your weapon today if possible, okay?"

"I will, and thank you," I replied, feeling chastised.

"See you later, Kelly." He furrowed his brow and walked out.

Ken jumped up as if on cue and walked toward the door. "Hey, I'm showing the love," he blurted out. "You know, that gun might save your life one day."

"Anyhow, the Carlson case is a go. I will follow up with the dad and brother today around 3-ish."

"Okay, Ken. We are taking on Kelly as a client, and I will certainly need some support on it," I said.

"Fantastic. I'm sure I will see you around then," he said to Kelly.

"Likewise, Ken," Kelly said with a dazzling smile.

He left, mentioning something about drinks this evening at the Brewery and to brief him on the case then.

After everyone had left, we talked a few more minutes about the case, and she stood to leave, mentioning that more work awaited her at home and the office. "Let me walk you out, and again, please don't worry about our fees. I'll get back to you on that."

"I really need to see where the preliminary investigation goes first," I said as we left the office.

I was thinking that the fees for this case might not amount to anything substantial because the case might not go anywhere, or so I thought. Those people in Portage, the sheriff's department... well, they don't like me. Actually, I believe they hate me.

We walked past Callie's desk. She looked up, covered the phone's mouthpiece, and said, "Goodbye, Kelly." Strange, I thought. She's never done that before to prospective clients, using their first name.

Kelly waved back and said, "Bye-bye." Hmm, I need to keep an eye on that woman.

As we reached for the door, a shadow suddenly blocked out the filtering light, causing her to momentarily jump backwards into my arms.

Chapter 21

Sitting directly across the parking lot from the office's front door, the shooter had a great view of the MRO office, the parking lot, and the surrounding buildings in this business district. He found himself quite amused at all the people coming and going, talking and listening. People-watching excited him, and on this fine and hot Saturday morning, so did singing.

"Bitch, bitch, bitch, bitchy, bitchy, bitch, bitch, what are you doing right now?" sang the shooter as he continued to surveil the front entrance to the office. What a grand office it was.

Business looks like it's booming—a new location and...

He momentarily interrupted his singing when he saw a large black man stop and enter the front door of MRO. It looked like some kind of commotion was going on in the doorway.

"Daaaamn, Herschel, you done gotten bigger, brother man dude," he said.

"I bet your big black ass it's got to do with lip-smacking soul food or steroids." Saying this caused the shooter to chuckle at his humor and wit. "Well, it would be nice to find out what was going on over there," he thought out loud.

But it probably had no important bearing on his current job at the moment—well, not the one he had just finished early this morning, he hoped. They were dead and would not be discovered for a while—quick, quiet, and done.

He was just now starting to feel the effects of the redeye flight. It was a quick turnaround. No one knew what he was doing here, not even the stupid assholes that hired him, and they seemed to be on a self-destruct mission, which he hoped would not implicate him.

As he continued to watch the doorway, he could see the big fella talking to someone inside, but not to whom—assumably Parker and the girl, one Kelly Ryan, he thought excitedly.

"Kelly Ryan! I'd like you to meet Tiny Jackson," I said, laughing.

We were all laughing, still standing in the doorway, recovering from literally running into each other.

She shot her hand out in Tiny's direction, still smiling, and replied, "Pleasure to meet you, Mr. Jackson."

Enclosing her hand in his baseball glove-sized hand and sporting a 2-million-dollar smile, Tiny replied, "No, little lady, the pleasure is surely all mine, and Tiny is the name. Please indulge me with this."

"Okay, Tiny it is!" she said.

"Kelly Ryan is a new client of ours, and I might need your expertise on some jurisdiction matters pertaining to her case, if you know what I mean."

Turning and winking at him, knowing that if it got dicey, he might have to cover my ass—make that save my ass—in his jolly deep baritone, he laughed and said, "I think I have an inkling of what you are suggesting."

"Well, please excuse me. I must go and see the all-mighty one about Styles," Tiny said, directing this at me.

"I already know what you mean. Later, T," I replied. "Good luck!"

We walked out the door toward her car, stopping, and she turned around to face me in the bright glow of the muggy morning sunlight.

Chapter 22

"Okay… it's been over an hour, and I am getting tired of butchering the lyrics to really good songs on the radio," the shooter thought. Not to mention sitting here in the staggering heat in a rental car that smelled like shit. Although the car had decent enough air conditioning, the smell of pungent stale cigarettes and old coffee permeated throughout it. Currently, he was destroying the lyrics to "Pig" by the Cleveland industrial rock band Nine Inch Nails—a song he liked quite well, though not in his current rendition.

"What do we have here?" he said in a singsong tone.

"It's about fucking time. Thank you, people," he spat joyously.

Exiting the building were a good-looking tall black man and a very pretty brunette. Maybe a bonus in all of this work. The man had an athletic build, about six feet one, maybe a little under two hundred pounds.

"PAAAARKEER…" he drawled out, smiling as if he had just won the lottery. Maybe he did.

"My boy, you are looking fit as a fiddle these days, young buck."

He laughed, thinking what he had just said was funny for some damn reason, and turned back to watching the two in conversation.

She squinted and said, "Thanks again, Parker, for looking into this for us."

"Not a problem," I replied, shrugging my shoulders. "Kelly, I just have one more question for you."

"What are you not telling me?" I said, looking her straight in the eyes.

"What do you mean?" she shot back, quite surprised.

"What I mean is I'm getting a sense you are not telling me everything you know," I said.

"Well, what I know is what I am telling you," Kelly responded, quite put upon. "I'm telling you there's absolutely nothing I forgot, Parker... I am sure of it."

"Is there something I said that is leading you to believe that I am not?" she asked.

"No... nothing like that, just got a feeling that we are missing something," I said. "I need to know everything you feel is important and pertinent to your brother's death. No matter how insignificant it might seem to you... that's all," I replied.

"Family members tend to protect their loved ones, so little things might be blocked out."

"Okay… yeah, interesting," Kelly said furtively.

They were engaged in what seemed to be a fairly good-natured conversation, if not an interesting one. From the way they looked at each other, one would suspect they had much more going on than just a business meeting, he thought.

"I wouldn't mind having something going on with that piece," the shooter remarked.

As he continued to observe, both looked in his direction, squinting from the sun, not noticing his nondescriptive sedan. They walked over to her car, talking about the lack of media attention the case got, stopping only as they reached the car's driver's side door and pausing for a minute. She then turned to face me and said, "Parker, you know that no matter what we find out… good or bad, Guy and Laurie did not deserve to die, period. You know this, don't you?"

I just looked at her, nodded my head in agreement, and thought, be careful, Parker, my boy. Be damn careful!

"I will call before Thursday this coming week to update you on anything pertaining to the investigation."

"Yes, that would be really cool," she said.

The shooter was still watching and taking notes, with more emphasis on Kelly.

"Daaamm! Girl, you got a nice set of long legs on you, and your poohter doesn't look half bad either," he said, licking his lips slowly to emphasize a tasty attraction to this thought.

"Okay, hon, it's been a nice hour... time to move," he whispered, looking at his Tag Heuer.

"Whoa ho ho... my bad. Make that an hour and a half. Shit, girl! Leave my boy alone."

"This man has a job, and I need to get some rest before checking into the office..."

The shooter was staring at the couple as if he was reading their lips in conversation, anticipating their next move. Climbing into her Audi, she put her sunglasses on and waved goodbye as she drove away.

"It's about time, dude. She's leaving. Wake the fuck up!" Slim shook Carl "Bang" Smitts.

The two had dozed off momentarily, not noticing that another vehicle nearby was watching too.

"Shit! Whoa, I got it," Bang said, shaking his head, looking in the Rearview mirror and the side mirror.

"Alright, it's on!" Adjusting his seat upright, he pulled out and almost hit a blue Ford sedan.

Parker was standing, shielding his eyes from the sun, and watching as she turned onto Bryandale Rd.

Thinking, damn, it's going to be another hot-ass day, and I'm not out playing.

He turned around just as a blue Ford sedan slowly glided by, braking momentarily as a grey Mercedes cut him off. Something familiar about the smiling driver made Parker follow the car as it stopped at the end of the driveway for oncoming traffic.

"Hmmm…" he said, walking back towards the front door and the craziness that wait inside MRO.

Chapter 23

Utah National Park Ranger Whip Jordan was out for a routine morning drive this Saturday when he decided to turn onto Route 44 West and head up to Mustang Ridge in Ashley National Forest. The drive this morning would be routine in the quintessential scheme of things, but with the events of the past two days fresh in his mind, HELL... EVENTS! Since when do you call a double murder an event? he chastised himself for casually dismissing it as an event.

Parking his five-year-old Ford Explorer, his own POV, at the trailhead instead of down at the visitor parking lot behind the Canyon Lodge, he stared deeply troubled through the dust-caked windshield.

Reaching across the seat, he grabbed a radio and his camo University of Washington Huskies football cap—non-government issue, a small discretion he allowed himself.

Climbing out, he shoved the radio into his jacket pocket and strolled up the Canyon Ridge Trail towards the North Canyon Ridge Red Trailhead and then over to the Red Rim Canyon Cove section of Mustang Ridge.

Whip, as everyone called him, was well-liked by all the rangers. It was not uncommon to see the tall blond man with grey-streaked hair out in the wilderness hiking around, talking to visitors. He was a man who enjoyed people, and people enjoyed him. He was always quick with a positive word and praise for all the rangers who worked under him as the District Ranger for Flaming Gorge Region.

In this position, Whip was required to perform many more administrative duties, but no one cared that he stayed out of the offices as much as he stayed in them, which was not much.

This morning, his normally quick-to-smile, tanned face of fifty years—though he looked to be in his mid-forties—wore a concerned mask of someone deeply mulling over a troubling dilemma.

From his unshaved face, his enigmatic blue eyes cast a tired gleam out ahead to the far side of the cliffs as he strolled along the canyon rim. He had forgotten in a matter of days just how beautiful this location was on the Gorge. Standing on the southeastern rim of the Gorge, he marveled as the rising sun's lonely shadow cast ghostly images that danced on the majestic golden and red canyon walls.

The piñon, juniper, and evergreen trees to the southwest and west grew down close to the azure blue waters and its coves throughout the ninety-plus-mile length of this pure treasure.

He thought of that morning like this one—no, not like this one, not peaceful and serene like this one. More ugly, violent. Finding those bodies, seeing the blood, what a damn mess, in my park, the finality of it all. The radio chirped to life, but it was not a call for him.

It was Ruth at dispatch calling on the service of another ranger for a location check. Turning, Whip kicked a small rock over the rim where he was standing, watching it sail down into the darkness. He thought of the investigation and the FBI's involvement.

How the Vernal resident office was called in from the home office in SLC, and then DC swooped in and took over the investigation from the state police. What a whirlwind couple of days. Abcrombie Fitzgreadal at the Vernal office was a nice enough fellow, and you could tell that he didn't think the case would remain in his hands. Hmm, he thought, something bigger is going on at the federal level.

The woman they brought in from the Cleveland office—what was her name? Caffeine?... No! Caferen or something like that. Helluva good-looking girl and a pretty sharp investigator.

She was honestly objective, unlike her tight-ass GQ-looking partner Kenneth Froom, who fit the typical bureau prototype. Now smiling as he thought of how Agent Cafren O'Malley would smile, then look away and find something in the park to point out to him, then ask his perspective on the situation. Smooth woman, he thought. Well, I'm a happily married man of 25 years, and Linda, my wife, would have my butt.

Whip looked down and kicked another rock, pausing, fixated, and intently focused on the toe of his boot.

He was standing over a little fissure crack that glided narrowly where he was standing and widened as it snaked toward the cliff. Protruding ever so slightly upward through the crack was a corner, just enough for Whip to catch his boot tip on when sliding his foot backward.

Stepping back and kneeling for a closer inspection, he saw leather! At first, he thought it was maybe a dead hide from a long-decomposed animal that was buried and covered over time.

Unclasping his knife sheath and withdrawing it, Whip set forth digging around and widening the crack until he was able to free the item. Taking a pencil from his pocket wrapping, he left it on the ground and used the end to open it up. Taking a deep breath, he sighed, wrapped it in a handkerchief, and put it in his jacket. Whip stood and looked around—the day just got more interesting.

Chapter 24

Jonas and Paul Lee were enjoying a beautiful lunch at one of the only three five-star restaurants he allowed himself to frequent. The Tango Room on the square is where the mighty and the powerful sit down to spar or just pose for attention at high noon or at dinner. Oh, and the food is excellent too. You rarely saw the same people during both of its equally busy dining times. Weekends had an entirely different flow, with brunch added to the mix.

Jonas loved to pose and preen at noon and seldom did dinner downtown, opting to frequent the more trendy and opulent suburban establishments. But on this lazy weekend, after schmoozing a couple of out-of-town visitors, he was feeling good—no, not good, fucking stupendous!

The Europeans were here to coordinate the exchange of the working prototype of the S.M.M.A.R.T. for their bosses. S.M.M.A.R.T. (Satellite, Missile, Microwave, Artillery, Remote Triggers) is a remote micro-guidance system for use with directed energy weapons such as Active Denial Weapons and Micro Electro lasers. The unit can be linked to your smartphone or worn as a watch, to control armed drones, satellites, missiles—anything that is computer-dependent.

He had developed the system for Sys-Tech. This was his brainchild for years as he worked his way up the corporate ladder, and then four months ago, they shelved it due to lack of funding. Now they wanted to start working on it again. Too late. He'd been working on perfecting it with the young engineers, which included Guy Ryan. Sorry, dude, he thought, you were brilliant. Fuck the lobbyist bastards working with Congress to shut them down, only to want back in. Too late, my friends.

The Air Force Research Laboratory and the U.S. Department of Defense were interested in the beginning, and after a few failed tests, the interest started to dwindle. Then the killer—no more funding.

Well, that has changed. With the renewed interest and financing from his new partners, he was able to test and build without anyone paying attention, thanks in part to his ability to deflect government interest towards his newer projects in development stages. He was on top of the world, his game was tight, and his bank accounts in the Caymans and the Philippines were too—one hundred million delivered to his and Paul Lee's account of choice. The visitors over the last two days were not just any old run-of-the-mill knuckleheads; they represented some damn powerful folks globally. The plan was to deliver the package at a neutral site, with his two new Euro buddies heading the exchange with their cohorts. The tests in Wyoming went off without a hitch; nobody suspected a thing. NSA, FBI, Air Force—no one was the wiser.

Dressed casually, he was wearing a pair of Jhane Barnes grey chino slacks and a yellow Ralph Lauren linen shirt, topped off with his favorite casual footwear, a pair of Cole Haan driving mocs.

During the workweek power grind, Jonas favored power suits, with his choices being Jil Sanders and Ermenegildo Zegna. He was a big-time mover and shaker by his estimation, a rising star on the fast track— that was his bosses' and colleagues' view of him, and they might be right. Others would simply suggest that he was narcissistic, an opportunist, vile, or just a plain old evil fuck.

No matter what you thought of his persona, professionally people tended to give him quite the respect or avoid him altogether. He liked to say that he grew up fast and desperate on the mean streets of Baltimore, when in fact, he actually had a sheltered and quite privileged upbringing in the town of Havre de Grace, north and east of Baltimore.

It wasn't like he was the good son wanting to have a gangsta rep; he was troubled and deeply so. This he knew, but what the fuck—the world was full of deeply screwed-up people. He was just a rich and intelligent one. His parents' influence and money got him out of some things. The psychologists and therapists helped, maybe. But if they only knew the horrible things that their little Jonas had done, no amount of political influence and money would help. But no one would ever find out. He had taken great care of this; it was not plausible to link him. The past secrets would stay buried deep—too many years had passed.

Shit! Why was he even thinking about the past? Hell, it was the now, and the past was the... past.

Reaching over to pick up his mimosa, his cell vibrated. Looking at the screen and then over at his brunch companion, he nodded and smiled.

"Good. We are expecting this call."

Chapter 25

"You fucking simpleton... you did what?" Jonas questioned in a low, controlled tone.

"Jesus... I told you to get information, that's all... not to kill her," Jonas said incredulously.

The voice on the other end of the Saturday afternoon call was filled with urgency.

"I'm... sorry, Jonas... I kind of lost my head, you know..." the caller said.

"You kind of lost your head!" Jonas repeated sarcastically. "You told me to work fast... that the FBI might be aware!"

"And... oh yeah! I'm sure they are..." Jonas let that hang in the air.

"She was a real snotty bitch!... Anyway... it's done. What was I supposed to do? She fought me."

"Marcella, did you at least find out anything useful... like where the package is?"

"Yes, I... believe so," Marcella replied.

"Good God, man, I hope for our sake," Jonas said. "Do tell me all the sickening details quickly now," he commanded, smiling.

Paul Lee looked at Jonas and knew that Marcella was recounting some horrendous event and that Jonas was taking great pleasure in it. He had known him long enough and had, on one occasion, seen what he thought was the psychotic side of this guy creeping out as he described what he'd do to a person he despised. Not a nice guy.

Marcella, in a hurried breath, recounted the brutal interrogation and rape of the previous evening.

"Slut!... She fought like crazy," he ended his recollection by saying.

"Interesting... hmm," Jonas purred as he luxuriated in the retelling. "Marcella... you are indeed one delightfully entertaining and sinister fuck!"

"Yeah... sometimes!"

"Hey, Jonas, should we be talking about this on the cell?" Marcella asked.

"Good damn question, now that you've told me everything. The cell is as secure as one can be for now. It's a throwaway. If it changes, you'll know. Alright, I suggest we meet and see what's what," Jonas said, raising his glass.

"Yep, of course. You at your old haunt?" he said.

"Yes, I am with Paul Lee," Jonas intimated.

"See ya in about twenty," Marcella responded.

"Perfect! See you then," Jonas replied and terminated the call. He took a long drink and smiled.

Paul Lee Raverstine was ordering another Bloody Mary when Jonas ended his phone conversation.

"Good choice of drink. That was Marcella. Good and more good news and a little bad... but not so much."

Paul Lee, as he liked to be called, is a powerful man in his own right at SysTech. As the number two man in the pecking order behind the CEO, Jim Masterson, he is as odious as he is conniving.

Paul Lee is a couple of years senior to Jonas and is quite a smart dresser like Jonas, he too got his start as a bio-computer engineer before moving to the business side of SysTech.

In a slightly annoyed and agitated voice, he remarked, "Who'd he kill now?"

The waiter had already gone when he said this to Jonas.

Jonas sighed and looked out at the beautiful array of flowers, some struggling, some flourishing in the heat of the outdoor gardens. Rhododendrons, irises, and hydrangeas all beckoned his gaze as he thought lazily about the circumstances of the call.

"A temp... who worked as a receptionist..." He looked over at the hostess leading a man and woman to their seats.

"Who now!... Marcella is enjoying it too much," Paul Lee said lazily.

"Well, she was friends with the others and mentioned that one had a sister named Kelly."

"Whoa!.. you better reel in your boy before he leads the FBI straight to us," Paul Lee responded, not the least impressed. It was not unlike Paul Lee to have a contingency plan in case he had to bail out, and right at the moment, he was thinking about it.

"Yeah, well, I got him in check, so there will not be any loose ends."

"million of reasons," Jonas smiled.

The waiter returned with the drink.

Chapter 26

"Marcella can't keep this shit up... killing, you know."

"Understandably, Paul... I welcome your concern, but you're wrong, he can if need be," Jonas replied.

"The question is; you may ask me... will I?... we will see." Jonas dabbed his mouth with a napkin.

"There comes a point in time when people... the authorities begin to suspect something," Paul Lee shrugged.

"All of the people in these deaths have ties to us, and the implication... would be such as..."

Shrugging again and holding his hands out as if for emphasis on the immensity of the situation.

"I am quite aware of the implications..." Jonas remarked spitefully.

"But I will do whatever is required to find out who all knows... and eradicate the sources, Paul!"

"Fine, Jonas! Just remember, your ass is not the only one in the frying pan."

"We need to keep a tight lid on this. You don't want the other players finding out, do you?" Paul Lee said as the waiter arrived with his drink and set it down with a napkin.

He turned and addressed both men, "Our lunch menu is available now! Mr. Habbas and Mr. Paul."

"Mr. Habbas, would you like another mimosa?" The waiter asked.

"Yes, thanks, Jimmy."

"Yes, sir, Mr. Jonas," Jimmy replied.

"Would you like me to put your order in now too, Mr. Jonas and Mr. Paul?"

"Sure, Jimmy. Why not? I'll take the roasted bell pepper cranberry chicken salad and some whole grain rolls," Paul Lee recited from familiarity, because it's what he always orders for lunch.

"I would like to have the smoked Pacific salmon salad with whole grain rolls as well," Jonas said, thanking him.

"Jimmy, there will be another gentleman joining us. Could you send him over when he gets here?" Paul Lee said and slipped him a twenty as he nodded his understanding.

Jimmy always liked to wait the table that belonged to Mr. Paul, as he called him, and Mr. Jonas. They were quite big tippers, and they knew that he would only come over when signaled. Unlike some of his co-workers, who would lurk around their table like vultures.

After Jimmy left to go get the drink and submit the food order, the two continued their conversation before Marcella arrived and the talk would have to be contained.

"So what's screwed up now? Or do I not want to know?" Paul Lee asked.

"Oh, nothing much. Marcella had an unfortunate lapse in judgment," Jonas said casually.

"And that equates to what for us?... No, wait! Before you answer... again, do I wish to know?" Paul Lee said.

"Hmm... Maybe... the girl knew the Guy dude and the bitch, she was a close friend of hers."

Paul Lee looked up at that precise moment and saw a familiar man gesturing in the direction of their table and realized that Marcella had arrived and with the help of Jimmy was procuring a drink before heading over to the table.

Marcella Lopez is an East Coast boy who grew up in the tough Cherry Hill neighborhood in Baltimore, in a working-class family, the complete opposite of Jonas's cushy suburbs. Marcella had to fight day in and day out for what he wanted. Marcella and Jonas have this unbreakable trusting bond that cements the two together as if they were blood siblings. Having come from two different backgrounds, the two could not be more alike. Although not an Ivy League graduate, Marcella attended graduate school with a degree in marketing from Johns Hopkins in Baltimore and a master from the streets of hard knocks.

Marcella ambled over, shook hands with both men, and sipped his drink, a red and gold concoction with umbrellas in it. A good-sized Hispanic gentleman, a little over six foot and well-built, with his dark complexion, this and his muscular stature, reminded you of a former baseball great.

"Hey, gentlemen, I like this place, but it's a little too stuffy for me," he said, showing a gold-capped tooth and a nice smile. "Not enough little Latinas dancing around," grinning still and simulating a salsa step.

"Please, you wouldn't know what to do with them anyway," Jonas remarked, laughing, pointing to a seat.

"Salsa my ass around them... dude!" he replied.

Laughing, Paul asked, "Want to order some food? I'll call the waiter over for you."
"Naw, I won't be here long, just wanted to tell you first that our little princess..."

"...Was a good friend of one Laurie R and that other girl, the one that had the climbing mishap."

"You have my full attention..." Paul Lee said, smiling.

Jonas was shaking his head and pursing his lips, agreeing with the story; he had a little information about Rebecca's accident. Marcella felt that they needed to know as little as possible and that he would handle all details and results. For this, he would bank a cool three million, just a homeboy looking out for one another. "According to the little lady, Laurie was boasting about having something that would blow

your company out of the water and if the feds got it, and Homeland Security got wind..."

"Well, let's just say that SysTech's punk ass would have hell to pay," Marcella continued.

"Well, what is it?" Paul asked, thinking that the problem was solved with the murders.

Pausing for dramatic effect, Marcella knew that they were hanging on his every word.

"A micro drive, with photos of you with some unsavory gentlemen of questionable nationality..."

"Known baddies from out of the country... and this, I presume, pertains to your new sat guidance systems."

"Shit!... that little mink... damn, she's got guts, I must say," Jonas smirked.

"Or had!" Paul Lee chimed.

"Where'd she take these photos and how?" Jonas asked.

"Don't know, haven't seen them?" Marcella gestured, turning his mouth down.

"But she confirmed who would have it... actually, maybe possibly one of two or both."

Marcella took a swig from his drink and set the glass down on the table.

"Mmm, that's nice," he said, looking at his cocktail.

Jonas picked the glass up and stuck a napkin under and said, "Please do tell... dude."

He did a sad slow drum roll and, grinning from ear to ear, looking like a drunk circus mime.

"One dead Rebecca Richmond, two dead Laurie Rice, three dead Guy Ryan, the boyfriend..."

"...was... mmm, collateral damage... Oops!" he said, shrugging his shoulders.

"Thing is we did Guy, Laurie was a bonus or vice versa." He explained.

"They both knew too much and so did this Brigette chick, deal done... move on."

"Well, shit! That really helps," Paul Lee listed out while turning to his left, making sure that the half dozen or so patrons didn't hear him.

Jonas was still thinking long and hard about this new development and did not seem to pay attention to this exchange between the two.

After what seemed like minutes, he said, "Okay, someone associated with these people has a copy."

"We just have to call in

 the resources, circle the wagons, and do damage control pronto."

"Hell, Geronimo! I thought that's what you've been doing," Paul Lee said sarcastically.

"Not to worry, Slick, Marcella to the rescue, there's more..."

"I took the liberty to check up on the Rice chick and the Ryan guy. He has a sis and she his only family to speak of maybe an older brother on the other coast, a lot older.

"Okay, Marcella, spit it out. I'm not in the mood to play guess what's in my head," Jonas smiled.

"That's it... I found out that they are close, it needed closer observation... so, I did."

"And... she has a copy... and I am currently working on the problem... as we speak."

"Well then... Gentlemen..." Marcella said, pushing back his chair and standing.

"I've got to get, so if you are happy with the direction, that we need to continue in to solve this matter..." Marcella paused then continued. "...then I will bid you adieu and move on it."

"Oh! yeah, don't worry about our little friend, she's resting over in PA. on the east banks of a river..."

"...pumped full of heroin, she's quite the party girl... I hear."

Both men nodded in agreement with his assessment, and seemed to have found some resolve in his handling of said problems.

"Good, we need that copy. Our delivery date is in the next few days," Jonas replied, standing and shaking hands. Paul Lee sat and waved, contemplating the situation before him.

When Marcella had left and the food had arrived, Paul decided to broach a subject that was troubling him. Taking a bite of his salad, he asked, "How much do you trust Marcella?"

"Just about as much as I trust anyone!" Jonas said, taking a bite of his salad. .....he's family.

Chapter 27

"Stop... Stop... Mmm... Cut it out, that tickles... Parker... Park, er... ooh!"

"That's my ear... Mmm... I see you're not going too... aah..."

"Keep nibbling on my ear... you'll regret it later!" She said laughingly, still not opening her eyes.

Opening the slits that I refer to as my eyes presented a slightly raging problem for my head.

Cringing at the bright sunlight filtering through my bedroom window blinds, I contemplated getting up. It feels nice lying in bed sore and at the moment intertwined with a lovely friend.

Laying here trying to remember all of the details from last night, I am greeted with the sounds associated with a peaceful Sunday morning. Chirping birds, car doors slamming, and the weekend warriors of the yards starting their lawn mowers. The sweet scent of perfume mixed with the intoxicating aroma of late-night sex starts to infiltrate and assault my early morning senses. This, in itself, is enough to start me on my path of realization that last night was not a dream. Hmm... I must be waking up...

The sensuous taste of a woman rests upon my lips... yes... last night was not a dream!

At the moment, a tan, shapely thigh is casually draped across my back with a toned arm resting above it.

Rolling over and opening one eye and then the other, which took a little effort to not wake my guest.

Laying before me in all of her splendor is a short mop of tousled dark sun-streaked hair, bed sheets askew, and the ever so perfect glimpse of Madison's rear.

She is facing the opposite direction and starts to mumble incoherently as I readjust my position in the bed.

Untangling myself from this beautiful mass of nakedness presents a new set of thought-provoking stimuli, and it's not with my brain. Should I stay or should I go? Damn, she looks good.

Oh... well, I need to get up, I thought. Delicately as I could, I disentangled myself completely from the blankets and Madison, silently! Or so I thought silently!

Madison started mumbling something again and it sounded like "Parker... stop it, that tickles..."

"Go figure!" I whispered and bent over and kissed her gently on the backside.

She would think that Bark licking her on the ear was me.

Moaning quite appreciatively and looking like it was soothing, I felt overmatched by a dog.

"Bark, get out!" I whispered quite jealously and gestured with my hand towards the door.

"Stop licking her... ear, boy... out," I said quietly with a little more venom.

It worked, leaving her to the bed and slumber, Bark and I ventured out for some relief and food.

Not noticing the time when I got up, there was a distraction, you know. What time is it?... 11:15. Damn, must've been a good evening, I smiled. "Alright!" I said, stretching.

Thinking about Madison Malloy upstairs and grinning slyly, I opened the French doors to let the dog out and felt the suffocating stillness of a tropical rainforest clawing at my every being. The humidity was stifling. I now understand why everyone was mowing their yards this early.

Grabbing a bag of Sumatra blend out of the refrigerator, I prepped the coffee maker and got Bark some food and fresh water. I started reminiscing about yesterday and last night. I had a busy Saturday, a new case had come my way, maybe! And I ended up getting picked up.

"Not bad for a Saturday night, Parker, my boy," I shrugged, hesitating to open the door and let the dog back in. He trotted over to his water dish and gulped and went back to the door. "Ok, dude, good luck," and out again he went. I may not have gone out if Ken and I had not been discussing the cases and watching Ohio State beating Rutgers football reruns. He insisted, and I was ready to celebrate a little that evening. Ken suggested drinks and dinner at the Brewery, and I did not refuse.

Chapter 28

The coffee maker beeped, snapping me out of my stupor as I stared off into the peaceful surroundings of my backyard. Pouring myself a cup and taking a peek out into the backyard, checking on the pup, he's good.

Moving to the living room with coffee in hand, I sat and started reminiscing about last night and how if Ken had not left me at the Brewery, Madison would not have ended up naked and in my bed, last night anyway.

I was so engrossed in thought about the new case at the brewery that I didn't notice Madison walked in. In all fairness, my back was slightly turned, watching the bartender's ass—her ass! She walked in and straight up to me. Pretty alert for a private investigator… huh!

Tapping me on the back, "Hey there, stranger, drinking alone."

Turning around, I stood and gave her a big hug and said, "Not anymore!"

Damn, she looked good! Really Good! Surprised and greatly happy to see her, it had been a long time, yes, a long time.

Waving the bartender over, we ordered a couple of Woodfords and chased them down with a couple of Barley God Ales.

"What's been up these days? It's been what, umm, a year since I've seen you."

"Nothing much, just work and the same old bullshit!" she responded.

Our drinks arrived, and she thanked the bartender and turned back to me and asked, "And You?"

"Working and Living and working," I mused. "Yeah, that's how we roll!" She laughed, moving hair out of her eyes.
I was starting to feel the effects of the two additional bourbons, and it was creeping up on seven o'clock, and the bar was starting to crowd in.

Madison hadn't eaten anything, so I offered to make her something back at my place in exchange for a ride.

"Deal!" she agreed! "Should we stop and pick up some wine?" She questioned as I tallied up.

"Nope, I believe I can handle that at the house."
I was gently jolted back to reality by a light peck on the top of my head.

This was followed by a slender yet muscular arm wrapping around my neck and then someone kissing my ear. Madison had apparently woken up and come downstairs as I reveled in my deep thoughts as to how we come to where we are… currently... smile!

She hugged me, climbing over the couch and then straddled me, being careful not to assist in spilling my coffee. Setting the cup down, I looked at her and said."Good morning lovely!"

"Good morning to you, handsome!" She said grinning and slyly looking me in the eyes.

Her medium-length hair was tousled and hanging again in her face, hiding the pert little nose and those big gray-blue eyes. I reached up and moved a few strands of hair back behind her ear, opening a curtain to her soul. Those searching eyes greeted me weary, worldly, and excited with my presence.

"Why did you get up?" she asked, pouting.
I looked over at the door and then pointed.

"You don't want to make an enemy, do you?" I said.
Bark was seated at the door looking in with his tongue hanging out.

She smiled and exclaimed, "Absolutely not Party pooper!"

Turning back around, she kissed me on the lips long and soft.

"You know, I had the strangest feeling that it was Bark licking my ear and not you."

"I bet if you ask him. he would more than likely agree."
I said and kissed her back.

"So…what are you doing today, Parker?" Madison asked slyly.

"Nothing at all. heck after last night, I'd say chilling."

"Sounds good to me, would you like some company?" She asked casually.

Smiling, I pulled her tight against me, "Nothing would be better." I said!

"Ok..Then let me get a cup of that delicious smelling coffee and take back to bed…"

Oh yeah, and it was delicious!

Chapter 29

Madison offered to drop me off at Belmont Porsche. This would work out great so I wouldn't have to worry about getting two cars back home or having to Uber it.

Madison and I had spent a wonderful Sunday together, watching old movies and just lounging around, getting to know each other a little more intimately.

It was cool; we decided to try and get together again if she could. She was in a semi-serious relationship with a hedge fund broker who lived in Cleveland and New York.

Hazy and humid was the morning, a great improvement over yesterday, and it looked like it might rain.

"What's up with the weather?" I asked her as she turned down Lorain Ave.

She shrugged her shoulders and looked out the driver's side window of her Volvo.

"Did you happen to catch the weather report while you were watching the news?" I continued.

"Part of it," she replied.

"Mark, the weatherman on channel 8, said there was a fifty percent chance of showers."

"Oh crap, great. I had hoped to get some riding in this evening if the case allowed it."

Madison dropped me off at Belmont Porsche, kissed me, and said that she would call me in about a week.

After dealing with the salesman for about 45 minutes, my car was ready, and I decided to drive down to Ravenna and pay an unannounced visit to my old and sometimes good friend, the Portage County Sheriff.

The drive should take me about an hour, and it would put some break-in miles on the car.

Merging onto OH 80, the Ohio Turnpike, I tapped the talk button on the steering wheel and called the office to inform Callie of my morning's agenda.

She informed me that Kelly Ryan had called and needed me to contact her about some new information that she might have pertaining to the case.

I assured her that I would touch base with Kelly, and she replied smartly that she believed that for the first time since I started working for the agency, that I indeed would.

"Also, we have a couple of new clients that we accepted over the weekend."
"Ken and John will be handling them at this point, with Razur and Tiny in support."

"Ok, I guess you will not need my help," I replied, happy to know that business was picking up.

"True. It seems like if the Ryan case pans out, you're going to have a lot to deal with."

"Yeah... Also, have Styles get with me. I can use him to do some scut work."

"As soon as he arrives, I'll relay your wishes," Callie said, sipping her customary latte.

"And good luck with Frankie... he does not seem too fond of you at the moment."

I agreed with her in principle. He doesn't like me at the moment.

Wincing, I concluded our conversation with an assurance that I would update her as soon as I finished my business down in Portage County.

"Good luck... huh," I repeated out loud to myself.

Turning onto Infirmary Rd, I relaxed and lowered the window, breathing in the fragrance of relaxing wildflowers, hay, and... new car interior. It doesn't get any better.

My thoughts drifted back to the impending confrontation that loomed just one right turn away.

Anticipating the possible hostility, I steadied my nerves by telling myself to chill, man, chill.

I did this all the way into the parking lot and started to say it again as I turned the car off but...

Looking straight ahead, I started smiling... my day just got good.

A blue Dodge Ram pickup was poised to gallop out of the parking lot with a 25' Bayliner in tow.

It's safe to say that there was more hop in my step as I walked towards the front door.

An older or more mature couple was leaving the building as I reached for the door.

"Good morning, young man!" the gentleman hummed.

"Ah, good morning to you too," I chimed back and held the door open for them as they exited.

Parker stepped inside the air-conditioned lobby and made his way back towards a cluster of offices.

A big-haired, dark-complexioned woman in her late fifties sat reading memos and organizing her desk. She looked up as he stopped in front of the desk.
"Delores, how are you, gorgeous?" Parker asked, employing his million-dollar smile.

Dolores Jennings, Frankie's watchdog of a personal secretary, smiled and pointed.

"He's in the back, sugar, and on his way to the lake, Parker," she replied, not smiling now.

"And your flattery will not get you anywhere, sugar. I'm married," she said, smiling again and pointing.

"Can't blame a man for trying."

"What kind of mood is he in?" I asked.

"Don't know right now... he's supposed to be off... but he was called in by Judge Jackson."

"Is he in there right now?" I questioned.

"Who? The judge?" She responded.

"Yeah!" I said, looking around her towards the office.

Frowning, she said, "No, hon, he's here to pick up some paperwork."

"But when he sees you, his mood will definitely go to shit," she laughed.

"Thank you," I said, turning my lips up and walking back to Frankie's office.

Chapter 30

"Oh! Crap... Cardinal, move out of my way," Cafren suggested, nudging the cat out of her way and almost spilling coffee on the floor in the process. Maneuvering around the caramel ball of fur and sitting down carefully, folding her tall five-foot-nine frame on the couch, Cafren let out a sigh of relief and took a sip of the black, steaming liquid. Monday was finally here, and not just any old one; this downtime was a well-needed one after a week of jetting out west for an ongoing investigation. The ideal plan was to bum around the house, maybe watch a movie or two, and of course, sleep.

She thought this was the perfect way to come down after an enervating week of work.

Pulling her just barely shoulder-length strawberry-blonde hair out of her face, she slid a scrunchie on, giving herself a ponytail on top of her head. Reaching over to pat the furball on the head, she smiled and asked, "Little guy, you want up?" An attention-starved and indifferent Cardinal obliged and climbed up into her lap, staring content and happily up into confident stormy blue eyes. "Well, little guy, how should we start the day off?" She stroked the cat's purring head.

"News or maybe a..." She turns and listens to the sound of clicking and the startup beeps emitting from the spare bedroom down the hall that serves as her office.

"Crap! I hope that's not who I think it is..." She said, dropping her head down and biting her lower lip. Hearing the voice, she kissed the cat on top of his head and said, "There goes my freaking day, thanks, Ed!"

Ed Rafferty stands and walks over to a large front window that looks out and down onto Lakeside Avenue.

The parking lot across the street is already starting to welcome its first inhabitant this Monday morning.

"Hmm, the start of another glorious day," he is thinking, perpetual motion, nothing ever shuts down, still holding the phone to his ear. Seconds earlier, he had just left a message for Agent O'Malley.

Rafferty is the S.A.C., the Special Agent in Charge of the Cleveland office of the FBI, a seasoned agent who is highly respected by his peers for professionalism and careful handling of top cases.

Still on the early side of his fifties, he radiates genuine strong caring confidence. Tall and blond with graying temples, his green eyes hold a tired weariness that has seen it all.

Reaching for the phone, he touches a button for a number already in the speed dial and waits, deep in thought. The wait is not long, a small yet commanding voice answers, "What is it?"

Summoning his exhausted thoughts back into some sort of logical order, he answers.

"Morning, C... got a new development on the McIntyre case!"

"Great! Now why today? I'm on a vacation day!" Cafren replies, pleading sarcastically, stroking Cardinal's head and knowing that Ed would make it up to her down the road.

"Came in hot last night, also we have another case that looks to be a dinger," Rafferty continued.

"Sorry, kid! That's how things flow in the bureau, I don't have to tell you. I will make it up to you."

"Agent Froom has been briefed, and he'll be back in from that training seminar today." He finished.

"Mmm..." She said, thinking he'll be all puffed up from his new learning experience at Quantico.

"Can you meet me downtown in an hour, brief you there," Rafferty questioned, waiting for a protest.

"Hell, why not..." She said sarcastically.

"Ed... I knew it was too good to be true," she replied coolly, holding back her grating displeasure.

"Sorry, C, duty calls, and you get to see your favorite guy again."

A small girlish laugh emote through the phone's earpiece followed by, "Oh yeah... Mmm huh."

Hanging up the phone and looking at the kitten, Cafren unfolded her long legs from the couch.

"Movie's on hold, guy, till later."

Walking to her bedroom, she was wondering if it was about some new development out of Utah on the Jim McIntyre case or a new case closer to home.

Smiling, she hopes so because it would be unbearable to go back out there again with the bonehead that went with her the last two times. Well, if nothing else and it pertains to the McIntyre case, it will give her a chance to spar with Parker again, something she enjoyed so much, and maybe solve this damn case. God knows it needs to be solved for the family's sake.

"Piss his ass off!" she thought aloud about Parker, walking into her closet and selecting a suit.

The 20-minute drive from her lakefront condo in Bay Village would give her enough time to mull over particulars on the case again.

"Thanks, C for coming in..." Rafferty said, pointing to a chair in front of his desk and walking over to the coffee pot. "Emma, please hold all of my calls, unless it's life-threatening," he says into the phone.

"You need a cup; it's going to be a long day for me!" He asked.

"Yes...?" Calfren replied, sitting down.

She had jetted out of the house clad in a dark blue Calvin Klein suit with a relaxed cut around her very slim waist. This allowed for her to carry her SIG Sauer P228 in a back holster.

Calfren also was known to carry an ankle holster with a P238. She was wearing a light blue shirt with grey pinstripes and a pair of Michael Kors sensible flats; of course, these were not great for running in, so she always kept a pair of running shoes with a quick-pull lace system available from her triathlete days.

Taking the coffee from Rafferty, she sipped and settled in for the update.

"Ok, what'cha got?" She asked, praying that a trip to Utah was not in the immediate future.

"I'll make this brief; everything is in the folder," he said, taking a drink.

"Ok, lady, two things... you remember Ranger Whip, don't you," he started.

Cafren nodded, feeling the dread creeping in, a plane trip with numbnuts out to Utah... ugh!

"Well, he found a key piece of evidence," Rafferty was saying as Cafren drifted back.

He went on to explain that this comes in part to the fact that Ranger Jordan was working on another case that was close to our missing person's last location. He explained to her that the local field office is helping out with the investigation into the current crime that occurred there and how circumstantial evidence has possibly linked the two cases together. The new case, he went on to explain, has political implications, with the Department of Homeland Security and the Department of Defense. Everything is in the preliminary stages right now... today! Rafferty stood and handed her a folder from on top of a large stack.

"Yes, I am asking you to look it over and give me some input."

"Since you have knowledge of the previous case, I'm asking as a favor," he smiled and stood.

"Oh yeah, Raleigh Keith from the field office in Utah is your contact out there; he's a good fella, a family man, and by the book," he continued.

"When you start reading, you will see that this case has a local connection to a major corporation here," he said.

"Which former Senator Paul Mirarck has a connection to... his son runs it, one Morales Mirarck."

"... and the D.O.D. and H.L.S and other Capitol Hill groups, this case could be explosive," he said.

"Also, be advised that your buddy has his hands in this somehow, a client... or something."

"... or maybe he just somehow stumbled into it, god only knows," Rafferty shook his head and stood.

Cafren knew what he meant by buddy... a potential problem of a huge magnitude.

"Ok, I'll check it out and get back," she stood, feeling a huge black cloud looming over her. Another case with her asshole partner, Homeland Security and DOD, and Parker; this just keeps getting better, she thought, walking to her car, smiling.

Chapter 31

Portage County Sheriff Deputy Frank J. Forsyth looked up from a stack of folders, and there was Parker standing in the doorway, grinning. "You've got to be kidding!" Frank Forsyth said with disdain.

He was looking at an old friend that he could live without at the moment, actually maybe for the rest of his life. "Lord, what did I do to deserve this on my day off?" He asked pleadingly.

Frank is a big man, 6'3" and maybe a biscuit shy of 270 pounds with a full-on blond buzz cut and a tan, chiseled-looking face. However, don't let the wholesome looks deceive you; the man can be as nasty as a hungry Arkansas razorback. So when he is asking for help from the divine one, well, it goes to show that he is indeed concerned. Parker took his question thoughtfully, dismissed it, and walked into the office and sat down on the couch located to the left of the desk.

Looking around, it was rather spacious digs for a county-appointed employee. Two windows displayed the wooded area and the parking lot in front of the building.

A large older oak desk was located in the center of the room, with a closed laptop perched in the center and a couple of file stacks sitting on the left corner, otherwise nice and orderly.

The wall directly behind the desk was covered in awards, diplomas, and photos with local leaders all smiling and mugging. Two small file cabinets were located over by a non-window wall also dotted with two photos of Frank and some guys, holding up a dead deer, elk, or some other antlered animal.

"Well hello Frank, I am glad to see you... seriously!" Parker responded playfully.

"Seriously, Parker... NOT!" He replied.

"No... ah shucks... really, what are you doing here on your day off?" Parker asked.

"How do you know it's my day off?"

"Lovely Doris told me."

"Doris, you're fired..." Frank yelled out to her but got no response.

Returning his attention to the stack of files, he replied, pointing at the stack, "Judge Jackson... you know the guy, his honor... your friend." He said with a hint of vinegar in his voice.

"And since you're here, should I call him for you?" He suggested, smiling.

"Oh hell no... no..." I said rather quickly.

Judge Paul Jackson is a strange little man, whom I hope to never see again in my life.

The Judge had the charges dismissed from a little mishap that MRO had in Portage County because he did not want the media circus to descend on his town.

Also, he felt the prosecutors lacked sufficient evidence to process the case in good conscience and that it was worthless to spend the taxpayers' dollars on a trial that was not going to help him on election day.

Although he did this little favor to avoid a possible embarrassment, Judge Jackson made a point to let me know that he would not, in the future, tolerate me or my firm causing unnecessary disruption or intentional compromising on an ongoing investigation in his jurisdiction. It was all good, and it works for me and the firm, totally!

Still, Frank did not look pleased to see me; I was quite sure he was no doubt still harboring ill will towards me for our past history together. "Dressed for success, I see," he remarked, curiously looking me up and down.

"Why don't you eye-rape me for god's sake," I reeled.

"Yeah... mmm..." He looked back at the files.

This has always been a point of contention with us. Frank and a lot of my friends and also former clients felt I could dress a little more professionally, and from what I hear, it might even actually impact the amount of business, in a good way. My answer to them was to go ahead and dress comfortably, like I was today, in my CK khaki cargo pants and my Timothy Everest blue button-down shirt topped off with a clean pair of Aslo GTX hikers; I looked smart, I thought. Adjusting my position on the couch, smiling, and knowing that I would have to one-up him.

"Modeling myself after a fashion god, such as yourself, is not easy..." I replied.

"Humph...if you say so...you could learn something," he grunted.

Dressed in cargo shorts and a camo T-shirt with the picture of duck feet sticking up out of a pond and the words, "Friends of Fowls" on it...

Sheriff Deputy Frank J. Forsyth, and I have what you might call an interesting history, which goes back a few years ago to what the Portage County officials call "The meth-lab fiasco," I called it "The little mishap." Ken, Rasur Gutierrez, and myself were working on a lead for a client and got some unsubstantiated intel and did not vet the source properly. So we had no idea that a couple of the client's family members were at the time under surveillance for running a large methamphetamine operation in Portage County.

MRO was just simply checking into a possible lead for my client, about a case of valuable art stolen by some relatives. Not in your wildest dream could you have imagined showing up to this house, to question the client's brother and having a shootout ensue.

The little detail of a full-fledged meth lab operation did not come up during the preliminary investigation.

Long story short, the lab blew up, and 2 people died.

It didn't matter that they were bad people with long rap sheets and a tendency towards violence.

They had been sampling the product all day and were pretty whacked out of their heads by the time we arrived. The fallout was huge, big time. Proper procedure, one of many charges if I remember correctly, was not followed. This is what I was told by all of the respective governing authorities.

Even though, as a common courtesy, the Sheriff's department had been notified before we showed up.

My bad! I guess a lot of folks with initials for department names got involved and were pissed off at MRO.

Well, at least MRO was mentioned in a few government circles and cocktail parties; I guess it wasn't that bad.

Maybe not quite the way Uncle Jim would want to hear or see us mentioned.

I thought that Frank would take a big hit professionally and politically on the blowback, guess not!

"You don't seem to be doing bad..." I said.

"It worked out... and I don't want to explain it after the fireworks died down."

"I can thank you at least for that... the blame..." He said.

Hell, I nodded a thank you in agreement. It's the least that I could do for making his life hell.

Chapter 32

"I got an itch, I got an itch..." The shooter sang as he sat waiting.

He was damn good at waiting, hell, he was the best at waiting if you were to have him tell it.

This morning would start out with a little job that needed tending to before work started.

There were times that he wondered why he didn't give up the office job; this was much more fun and exciting. Besides, the client was a lucrative one that's provided him work in the past.

His Cayman bank account was impressive; one would marvel at its diversity.

Today's gig is what he called an appetizer before the main course.

And the time was not right yet, too much work to be done, too much fun to be had before that meal.

"Let's see, I need to kill somebody today, and it tisss... you."

Looking up from a map that he was pretending to study, the shooter locked onto a car approaching the four-way intersection. He was parked at a gas station, directly across and to the left of this intersection.

So the target car turning left would have to go right by him.

This he knew from previous research of the prospective target, and of course, his intel was spot on.

At last, the light changed, and the silver Mercedes shot around the corner.

"Oh yeah!... Let the games begin."

Smiling, he put the map aside and moved the car out into a stream of traffic.

Following at a distance of three cars, it's not likely that the target would recognize a tail.

He followed the car as it sped up, crossing over two lanes heading north on Rt 77 and towards downtown Cleveland. Accelerating smoothly around a slower vehicle, the shooter closed the distance between the two cars quickly. Now it was important to stay at least two cars back until the final 1/4 mile, and then a one-car distance would be needed. Grant and the Harvard Rd exits zipped past, with a minimal amount of commuter traffic merging on. Merging over the right two lanes, the distance had to close quickly to one car in length.

The 480 exchange loomed ahead, and there would not be a second chance.

Looking back to check on the coming cars, the shooter overplayed his move and didn't see a Mini shoot over behind him, merging right. As he caught the speeding mini car out of the corner of his eye, he calmly accelerated left back out into traffic and around a slower-moving car.

The defensive maneuver was quite impressive, and he didn't lose too much of his position on the target car.

The distance with a half of a mile was one and a half cars. "Shit... What the fu…"

Baaaaa..vooroom, the sound of a motorcycle zipping past and in between the two speeding cars.

This happened so unexpectedly fast that it caught the shooter by surprise. "Shit...this won't work," he said aloud.

Calmly anticipating the options now presenting themselves before him, it was do or die time.

Calling off the hit was the smart thing to do or try to do, the biker and the target in one move.

It was too risky and not needed; no collateral damage, besides, he didn't kill innocent people unless they pissed him off. Abruptly, as the motorcycle had cut in between him and the target, the damn thing sped up and veered left around the target and accelerated ahead.

The silver Mercedes signaled for the exit right, and the shooter's blue sedan edged closer, nose to tail.

Half a car length is all that separated the two, and the damn motorcyclist had already hit the split and was headed onto I 490 West. Reaching this crux in the road, the shooter made his move and pulled around the now-slowing Mercedes. Knocking the map off the seat, he pulled out the Glock and raised it as the two cars pulled abreast of each other. The other driver didn't have time to register the situation.

In the moment that he looked over, the shooter pulled the trigger.

Phit, phit... two quick hits, and the driver side window exploded into a crimson pinkish blur.

"I guess you pissed someone off," he smirked. Continuing left with the contour of the road, the shooter looked into the rearview mirror and saw briefly the last glimmering bulk of the large silver car gliding down the embankment. With that done, it was time to head due south and then east to Portage County.

"What the fuck!... was that..." Styles said aloud into the foam of his helmet as he accelerated into the turn.

Having just sped past two slow-moving cars, slow by his standards which is a cruising speed of at least 85 mph. The blue Ford sedan had a flash inside of it, and then the big silver car driving off the side of the road, or so he thought, it was hard to tell because of the speed at which he was traveling.

He was headed to work and running late this morning; depending on the workload, he might hear about this after his last indiscretion. Drifting back to the previous thought, he said "…It could have been the reflection of the sun…" Bringing his attention back to the road before him and gassing the throttle hard.

Merging onto the road behind him, the blue sedan accelerated.

Chapter 33

"So, Parker, again I ask: what do you want and how's it going to affect my life?"

Not being in a serious hurry to answer his question because I knew the longer I put this off and held him up from going to the lake, the better chance I had of getting what I came down for or possibly pissing him off and getting nothing.

"I see the boat's all hitched up...where are you going fishing?" I asked, still ignoring his question.

"Yep, it is, and West Branch is the place," Frank replied.

"You know it's going to rain today?" I said.

"So I heard... Parker..."

"Oh!...and how come you never invite me fishing?" I asked, pretending to be hurt.

Frank looked at me long and annoyingly, "Ken, yes... you... No!"

"Well... Frank, I'm hurt," I replied.

"Somehow, Parker, I'm sure that you will recover."

"Now what in the SAM HADES! Do you want?" he said, agitated.

"The Guy Ryan and Laurie Rice files," I said with my best no-bullshit look.

Frank sat back in his chair and studied me, frowning as my words seemed to hang in the air.

"What's that got to do with you?" he questioned.

I explained to him that Kelly Ryan was a client of MRO and that we are looking into the murder of her brother. She's been unhappy with the lack of information provided to her in solving her brother and Laurie Rice's murder. "Her words, not mine," I so kindly pointed out quickly.

"The client in question also felt that all of the investigative resources were looking in the wrong direction," I continued.

During my explanation, Frank sat quietly listening with the same painfully shitty frown on his face.

When I finished, he casually asked, "And what direction would that be?"

"I can't divulge that because I don't know myself, Frank."

"But she is persistent in looking into her brother's death," I added.

Looking out the window, he stood and pulled his pants out of his ass and said, "Bullshit, Parker!"

"The case is... what! four days old... give me a break!"

"Frank, my firm is not cheap, besides, I know Guy Ryan or did know him."

Turning around quickly, he said, "You know who... what in God's nation are you talking about, Parker?"

"I could bust your evidence-withholding ass!" he snorted calmly.

Oh, and how you could, big fella, if you only knew what my client has in her possession, I thought, remembering those pictures.

"Chillax, big guy, let me explain; this I can do quickly," I said.

"Guy Ryan went to school in Virginia too..."

"... and we crossed each other's paths from playing on the same university lacrosse team."

"That's how we knew each other; I was an outgoing senior, and he was an incoming freshman," I explained.

I kept tabs on the team in the years following my completion of law school, and Guy was still playing.

However true this was, I would occasionally go out with Guy and the rest of the team for beers.

But it would not serve any good purpose to inform him that I had drunk a few times with Guy during law school and a couple of times when I returned from active duty in the Air Force reserves; not even Kelly needed to know about that. It also was true that I had not realized Guy was one of the victims in the West Branch killings. Sitting back down in the chair with a whoop sound and rubbing his face with his hand, I could sense and see the wheels turning in his head.

It's times like this that it's good to know when to speak and when not to, and now was a good time not to.

Rubbing his temple with a thick knobby forefinger and thumb, the cop in him wanting to bust my ass for not coming forward with this information, but also realizing that I didn't, in fact, know about the deaths before being hired to investigate the case as I explained.

"Here's the deal: I believe what you're saying... but it's still an open investigation," he said.

Holding up his hand to signify that he was not done talking, Frank continued.

"... And we are actively looking for leads and doing everything we can with the evidence that we have."

"We are waiting on the ballistic test... from the state lab, and we have submitted it to the FBI for comparison."

"As you know, these things take time; we put a hurry on, like all cases involving shootings."

"So we are working... contrary to your client's belief... Parker, so give me a break," he blew out air after finishing.

"And I will need to get a statement from you on any info pertaining to this case."

He reached for his phone and was about to call someone when I said, "Wait! I'll give you what I got..."

"... In exchange for something..."

Not moving from the couch, I leaned up with my hands on my legs and said, "Can I get your case files?"

He just stared at me with that non-expression look.

"Now, with that said, I have a lake waiting for me," he stated.

"You are welcome," I replied, knowing that he just agreed from the expression, no blowback to him.

Frank pushed his hulking frame up and out of his chair and walked around the desk over to the two filing cabinets and extracted a thin file and handed it to me.

"Don't let it leave this office, and do not let anyone know that you saw it...do we have an understanding?"

I nodded in understanding and agreement. "Yeah..."

"Doris, make sure Parker here does not leave my office with anything... shoot him if you have to."

Doris shouted back "with pleasure..."

"And get someone to take his statement before he leaves," he said, breathing out hard and staring at me.

"Parker, I expect you to keep me abreast of any new information...pertaining to the case," he said, giving me one file and keeping another one.

I nodded again, reaching for the file and said, "Thanks."

"Yeah, don't let it bite me in the ass..." Frank asked in a low voice.

"Well, I've got a lake to get to; as always, it's been a pleasure!" Walking past Parker and tapping on the wall.

With Frank out the door and on his way to the lake, I started reading and looked for the copier.

Chapter 34

A still muggy and ominously overcast mid-morning greeted me as I walked out to the parking lot.

"Man, it's going to rain and rain hard," I thought, looking up at the sky. "We could probably use it."

I made my way across the lot to my still-warm car. The meeting had lasted a little over an hour. Heck, it felt a lot longer, but in the end, I got what was needed for me to start investigating—or what would make it a little easier, I hope. Giving Deputy Taylor my statement was quick and concise, only what I thought he needed to know. Reaching down, I grabbed the door lever and was in the process of climbing in when I recognized an individual climbing out of a car parked two rows in front of me, looking away in the opposite direction.

I walked over. "Hello," I said in my most non-threatening tone, especially when coming up from behind someone. It didn't matter; she jumped anyway, whirling around looking quite startled.

"PARKER!... Oh my god!"

I didn't waste any time waiting for an answer before launching into my question.

"Kelly, what are you doing here?"

Regaining her composure, she smartly replied, "Trying to get an update from your Sheriff friend."

When I had walked over, I put my hands behind my back and still had the copies of the files shoved down the back of my pants, and now they were slipping down towards my ass, and I was starting to sweat.

Got to get them out, get them out. There was an awkward moment of silence as I contemplated what she said and the steadily creeping copies of files.

"Hmm... Well, Frank's not in the office... You missed him," I said.

"Did you get a chance to see?" she asked.

"Why, yes, I did, and it was...shall we say, interesting to say the least."

"You really do not want to keep a man from the lake, let me tell you," I said.

Kelly smiled and was about to comment on what I had just said when her face took on a somber note, turning away and gathering her composure before saying that she was going through more of her brother's stuff Saturday. A package had arrived delivered by a local mail carrier Saturday, addressed from her brother and mailed on Thursday to me.

She had not viewed the contents and thought that I might want to see it. She called the office this morning to inform me of this new development.

"When were you going to call me back?" she questioned.

"So, what was in the package?" I asked, not answering her question and thinking about what she had just shared with me and how the complexity of the investigation could change pertaining to the arrival of this package. Crap! Here we go with the custody, chain of evidence, and withholding stuff.

"I did not open it. I wanted to give it to you first," she said, looking me in the eyes.

The paper was still shifting around in my ass, and I was starting to sweat more. Do something quickly, I thought, gotta get to the car quickly.

"Uh... Where is the package right now?" I asked, moving my feet.

"At my condo... Would you like to see it?" Kelly replied.

"Yes, right away," I said, looking at my watch, wondering where the morning went. It was approaching noon.

"Should I bring it to you, or do you want to go to my place?" she asked.

Thinking again about the files sliding down the back of my shirt and not needing to stop at the office...

"Tell you what...your place. I need to call the office and follow up on some info about the case."

"Frank helped us out, I think," I said, turning to walk to my car.

"So you did talk with him..." she said, surprised.

"Yeah, I did. I'll tell you about it at your place."

Chapter 35

The torrential rain pelted the steaming blacktop with such velocity, causing the spray to rise up like amusing cataclysmic clouds of vapor. The rain had come, and come it did.

Driving back from Ravenna, I followed we had hoped to beat the impending storm, but that did not happen.

Thirty seconds after exiting off the shoreway onto Detroit Rd, BOOM! The skies opened up on us, just 500 feet from her home. Wet and... well, wet, we hurried into her spacious condominium, located on the far west side of downtown Cleveland in an area called the Detroit Shoreway neighborhood.

Perched on a hill looking out over the shoreway with a direct line of sight to the marina north on Lake Erie and the downtown skyscrapers to the east, and the beautiful tree-lined coast suburbs to the west.

It's a nice area of mixed ethnically old families and young professionals wanting to be close to the action and nightlife of the city. I stripped off my shoes while she hurried into a closet and returned with a small stack of towels. Taking one, I thanked her and took in the expansiveness of her large loft: vaulted ceilings, open floor plan, and quite a bit of extensive natural light, although today it was muted.

She beckoned me into the kitchen area, separated from the living room by a double-sided fireplace.

"Would you like something to drink, coffee, tea, juice, or something stronger?" she asked, grinning.

"Hmm... coffee would be fine," I replied playfully.

"It will be ready in a minute. I need to get out of these wet clothes. Sorry, I don't have anything to fit you."

I shrugged my shoulders and gave her a look that must have suggested that I did not mind wearing what I had on. She stopped and waited for me to respond. I said nothing. "Ok, then, tough guy," she said, and went upstairs. Toweling my head and shoulders dry, I stared out at what must have been an amazing view of Lake Erie and the downtown skyline at sunrise and sunset. Not so much of one at the moment.

Unlocking the balcony door, I went out and viewed what looked to be boaters down at the Edgewater Marina running towards the cover of the clubhouse, and a very wet man exiting a car and running towards one of the buildings.

Chapter 36

The alluring smell of good coffee wafted out from the kitchen, bringing me back to the moment.

Turning around, I walked back into Kelly, who was standing behind me. I hadn't heard her approach.

She had changed into cargo army green shorts and a Cleveland State t-shirt. Her hair was wet and pulled back into a ponytail, and she was still wearing a little makeup.

She looked good, and she was holding two cups of steaming hot coffee. They looked good.

I took one and thanked her. She said playfully, "You were lost in thought and smiling... I hope it's not the weather."

"Hmm... good cup of joe and yes... and no, not the weather..." I smiled.

Laughing, we both stood and stared at the transparent curtain of water that held us and many others captive under shelter. "You know, it's beautiful normally..." She said and took a sip.

"Yeah... I believe normally. Your neighbor probably didn't think so; he got drenched!" I said.

"Oh, he's back! Good, that means I don't have to watch his cat. The cat hates me," she said with a frown.

"Are you ready to look at this?" She asked, blowing exasperated air out.

I nodded and took another sip, checking her out over the rim of my cup. She did indeed look good.

"Let's go back in, and I will get the package for you," she said, turning and opening the door.

Following her in, I asked, "How long have you been here?"

"Two years... I bought it when they first went on the market. Got a great deal from a developer friend of mine."

"Well, you have a very beautiful place. What's the square footage?" I asked, sitting down at the kitchen counter as she gestured.

"1700 sq. ft.," she said, pulling a medium-sized FedEx envelope out of the kitchen drawer and placing it on the counter.

"Hmm...?" I said, using my keys to slice through the packing tape as Kelly reached for a letter opener.

Turning the envelope over, I shook out the contents onto the counter. A micro-drive black pouch fell out. I picked it up and unzipped the bag. Inside was a 2.4GB micro-disk and adapter.

Kelly walked over to the couch in the living room and returned with a MacBook Pro, placing it on the counter. "Well, let's see what's what," I said, picking up the laptop and placing it in front of me.

Kelly was quiet the whole time. She seemed to be mulling over the seriousness of why Guy would send her this package. Sitting down next to me, we opened the MacBook that was sitting on the counter and hit the power button. She smelled good, like coconut and vanilla. Moving in closer, she pulled the laptop back over in front of her and smirked. Humming and tapping in a smooth, rhythmic fashion, she went to work fast, gliding her smooth-looking hand over the keys and tapping in the password.

"Damn?" she looked up at me, confused, and continued humming and typing. "Something wrong?" I asked.

"Oh no! You probably now know my password, and I just remembered that I needed to change my neighbor's cat's litter box. Oh well!" she said.

The MacBook lit up, and a brighter image filled the screen with icons spread across the lower dock.

"Nice screensaver," I replied, focusing back on the desktop.

"Yeah, it is. Guy and me at Kelly's Island back early this summer," she said, biting her lower lip and contemplating it. "Okay, now what are we looking for?" she asked, sighing and turning slightly toward me.

Chapter 37

"Is this shit ever going to stop?" he thought as the rain continued to beat down on the front windshield of the Mercedes C63 AMG. He sat there uncomfortably for the better part of an hour, watching the condo through rivulets of beaded raindrops gliding down the car's windshield.

This is not an easy thing to do when the humidity is high outside and the windshield fogs up when you turn the car off. Not only was he wonderfully uncomfortable sitting stagnant and wet, but his fat-ass partner, who was also wet, fumbled with the front door lock of the condo, not worrying about who was watching.

The woman, Kelly Ryan, had just arrived home with that Parker P.I. dude about 10 minutes ago, and Carl jumped out of the car, not wanting to wait any longer.

Jimmy "Doc" Donavan was always up for making a few extra bucks, and Marcella said that he could make a quick thousand slot-ties for running over and picking up a package, a quick B&E, with no one getting hurt. Jimmy had a nagging feeling this was about to change because of the stupid fuck that Marcella had sent with him to retrieve the mysterious package from the woman's house.

Carl "Bang" Smitts was a big, loud man and a racist who constantly touted his abilities with the ladies and his powerlifting skills. Bang, as he liked to be called, had watched the woman a few days ago with Slim when she visited the investigative agency. Marcella used him quite a bit with some of his other crew, but it was Jimmy's first time working with the schmuck. The dude was also carrying a gun, a loaded .45, and was, in all of Jimmy's accounts, ready to use it. Shit! This, in my estimation, was not good at this location.

Jimmy was not opposed to the use of firearms; hell, he kept an Ithaca 12 gauge ultralight Model 37 with a pistol grip stock and two pistols, an M&P 40 in his home and a SIG P239, in the glove box. But his usage was reserved for high-velocity type situations, not this grab-and-go crap.

So it was safe to think that he might be in for some deep shit with this yahoo.

"Ah well, deal with it... and ad-lib... my friend," he said aloud to himself as he ran the current situation around in his head. Bang was not someone that he enjoyed being around, plus the guy was weird-looking. I'm just saying, he thought. But the guy got results, and Marcella was paying the bill.

"Well, let's wait and worry," he thought, laying back in the seat and adjusting the height of the open driver's side window to let some air in.

His current position allowed him a perfect view of the front door and the garage of Kelly Ryan's unit, not to mention a relatively quick exit if needed. He let the car idle just in case.

Chapter 38

She reached over, still focusing on the computer screen saver, and I handed her the micro disk and adapter. Assembling the two items together, Kelly inserted them into the USB port, and a few seconds later, the micro disk icon appeared on the desktop. "Well, let's see what's what," she said, finally looking over at me.

I guessed she was having a moment thinking about Guy, and the screen saver was the catalyst for triggering her emotions right then because before clicking on the icon, she paused, looked down, and said, "I'm sorry...just had a flashback looking at the picture again."

"We were drunk and ... happy," she clicked, and a slew of thumbnail shots of pictures filled the screen.

Fifty or more vacation pictures featuring two women on the beach, at dinner, on a boat, sightseeing, and what looked to be in front of a luxury beach house.

"Click on the beach shot," I said, pointing to one that had two women standing in blue water covering their ankles and a blue-gray horizon behind them; both wore bikini tops and sarongs. "Nothing like going straight for the flesh shots, hey," Kelly said, looking back up into my face as I looked over her shoulder.

"Yeah... who's who?" I asked, looking at the very attractive pair, ignoring her sarcasm.

Kelly clicked on another picture that had a caption under it, taken at a restaurant for dinner.

The women were dressed in a casual manner, sundresses with their hair pulled back into ponytails, and each had glasses of wine. There were about eight pictures in this manner, each with the women shot from different angles and with more of the restaurant patrons in the background.

"My guess, based upon Guy's description, Laurie is the blonde; I never got to meet her, unfortunately."

"And the other one... with dark hair, is a friend or co-worker, is my guess, maybe Rebecca," she intimated.

I got up and walked over to the balcony window, looking out at the street. It was still raining as I thought this out. "Yeah, you are correct about Laurie being the blonde," I frowned.

I didn't want to explain that I saw the crime scene photos, unless she asked, which she didn't.

"Okay, but what is so important that this was sent to you by your brother? It looks like friends vacationing," I said, watching. There was a gray car parked across from the entrance to the condo complex, with its wipers running and its parking lights on. Normally, I wouldn't read too much into it, but if my memory serves me correctly, it was this car that I saw a man running from, and it was this car that pulled in as we were walking into the building, and it's still out there running. "I don't know," she blew out air.

A knock at the door broke the seconds of silence; she jumped up and said, "My neighbor's not home..he would have called already."

Shit! Not neighbor, I thought, something is not right; I could feel it.

"Kelly, wait!" I said, grabbing the USB drive out of the computer and closing the top. "Kelly! Wait!"

It was too late; she was twisting the doorknob to open it, letting something, someone in... DAMN!

The door exploded inward with such velocity, Kelly was not given any time to avoid the brunt of its impact. She was caught square on her left shoulder and catapulted backward over an easy chair and into a lamp table, narrowly missing the wall with her head. She didn't move.

Chapter 39

Looking up at the door as I ran over to Kelly, I saw the long, black, ominous barrel of the gun first - a big gun! A gun that could, would do some damage - a lot of damage, in fact, a .45 H&K pointed at Kelly as she lay motionless not more than five feet from me. Reacting, I moved towards her and was commanded not to move any further.

"Not so fast, my friend... I believe you have something that belongs to a friend of mine."

A piggy voice sneered behind the gun; the voice didn't match the bulky figure that was standing in the shadows of the doorway. Focusing for the first time on the emerging bulk as he walked into the dim light of the living room and closed the door, I did not recognize him.

"She's hurt; I need to check her," I said, hands still in the air and moving slowly towards Kelly.

He was standing just inside the door with the gun still pointed down at Kelly, aiming at her chest.

The guy was big, like a bodybuilder gone wrong on too many steroids; it was muscle on top of a fat stomach and proportioned all wrong.

The guy was massive all around - arms, legs, shoulders, chest, and a belly - except for one thing.

His head was so damn small, small like a little kid's head on a grown man's body - small!

It was freakish, not an amusing thing to look at, just weird.

He was still looking at me, no expression, just looking at me with small black beady eyes in his small head. As if I was not getting it, displeasure registered on his face, and he pointed the gun at me now.

Big body flexed, turning his small freakish head, and with a piggy voice, he said again, "You have something that belongs to my friend..."

He was pointing the gun at me still, and just that quickly with his left foot, he kicked Kelly in the side hard.

She moaned and rolled over and balled up, moving her leg, and he kicked her again, not as hard this time, more of a taunt. "Ok... Ok... Ok! Don't do that again, just tell me what you want."

"What I want... is what I just said! ...the package!" He sneered through gritted and clenched teeth.

Kelly was starting to sit up, and I thought he would kick her again, but that was not the case.

"Put her on the couch first; I might want to have some fun with her if you don't honor my request."

Dropping my hand, I rushed over to her side as she seemed to struggle to remain sitting.

"How are you doing?" I asked, dropping down to my knees and steadying her with my arm around her back.

I could see that she had a bruise starting to show on her left cheek and a scratch on her chin, possibly from hitting the table. "I don't know... I hurt," she said and winced.

She dropped her head down to look at her hand, which was starting to swell.

"Ok, you and the bitch, move over to the couch," he said, using the gun to illustrate.

Kelly stood up, confused slowly with my help. Pausing and gathering her senses, she moved to the couch under her own power. We sat down on the couch as our guest kept his big gun trained on both of us, wondering what was next. I was trying to anticipate the next move - his and mine.

He quietly stared at us, not saying a word. I could see that he was thinking hard, concentrating, anticipating his next move, maybe! Keeping the gun trained on us and unclipping his cell phone from its case, he speed-dialed a number and waited.

"Yo, I got the two of them, and they are playing stupid... What should I do?" he sneered and then listened.

Looking around with piggy eyes as he listened and then stopping and coming to a focus on the kitchen counter and smiling. "Wait, I think we found what we are looking for... Yes... Bye."

Our captor pointed at me and then gestured with the gun towards the counter.

"Get up, man, and bring the laptop over here, and you, pretty girl, get up and come over to me," he said.

Clipping the phone back on his waist, he waved the gun at Kelly in a come-over-here gesture.

"I'll get what you want; she's hurt, can't you see?" I said.

I squeezed Kelly's leg and got up, looking her in the eyes hard, hoping that she knew that I had to do something, anything, be prepared. "Shut the fuck up, dude!" he shouted quickly.

She didn't move right away, causing him to repeat himself.

"You get your ass over here, before I shoot you in your fucking head... NOW!"

Apprehensively, Kelly stood up from the couch and moved towards him, as I turned and started back with the laptop. Kelly was standing directly in front of him, gun pointed at her chest, staring at him, not wavering. He reached out quickly, grabbing Kelly's hair and pulled her into him, placing the gun up to her head. "Now if you do anything stupid, I will put her face all over the room," he said into Kelly's ear, looking at me, moving his hand down to her breast and started stroking it.

Kelly remained impassive, but her eyes pleaded for help. I had to do something.

"Ok... Ok... Hey, here's what you came for! Take it and leave us alone," I said, walking towards him. Five, four, three, now two feet. In everyone's lifetime, there are moments when you feel like the dregs of uneasiness, a curtain or a cloud enveloping you like a stifling, choking darkness. It might paralyze you, you might cover up or......

Chapter 40

Marcella had just ordered another mojito and was settling in at Johnny's before getting the concerning call from Johnny "Doc" about that damn Carl Smitts charging up into the house. Now he was looking down at his phone again, waiting for the second time within a minute, and this time it was the dumbass himself... Carl. "Yes! What is happening..." Marcella asked, frowning and dreading the answer.

Listening for what seemed like five minutes, yet it was only about two, Marcella turned his back away from someone walking past his table.

"What do you mean two of them and playing what stupid? Persuade them, I don't know, beat their asses," he said to Smitts, annoyed.

"Wait... Wait! Never mind, look for a computer or a package that was just delivered."

"Ok, grab it and get out... quick, don't mess around!" Marcella disconnected and sighed.

Taking a deep pull from his drink and wiping his sweating forehead with the ice-cold glass, he turned on his stool, looking at the front door, and thought to himself, "This has the possibility of turning into a mess, and the man doesn't need to know about this at all. Jonas doesn't need to know about this at all." Turning and setting his glass down on the counter, he got up to go and relieve himself, waiting for an outcome that was favorable and he would have the computer. Whatever happened to those two at the woman's home didn't matter much to him or Jonas.

Parker was now close, within striking distance close, he thought, reaching out to hand the intruder the computer. He felt like a child handing back something forbidden that he had taken from his parents without permission. One more step, Oh! God NOOO! His brain was screaming as he felt his left foot catch on the table that was displaced when the guy busted in; his body darted forward, the computer leading the way in his outstretched arms. Surprised at seeing this intruder, the man lunged back as a natural reaction... to get out of the way and stumbled, grabbing Kelly, who moved forward and to the left, breaking the light grip that he now had on her throat.

She stumbled forward, landing on her knees, with the couch absorbing her impact.

Standing quickly and turning around, she saw Parker bring the laptop down, striking the big man in the face. His gun was still in his hand, and he was attempting to bring it up. Parker was to the left of him, smashing the laptop into his head for the second time when he saw the gun hand moving up. Kelly was running towards him and the man, who was trying to turn on his side.

Dropping the laptop, Parker swung this time with his fist, glancing off the man's smallish head as he moved it in an evasive sideways manner. He countered with his left hand, catching Parker's right shoulder momentarily, knocking him off balance. The intruder was scrambling to get up, causing Kelly, who had attempted to stomp the hell out of his freakish tiny wrist. Regrouping, I did what I needed to do, call me foolish, but I launched myself at him like a heat-seeking missile, using my forehead as a battering ram.

In other words, I headbutted the bastard. His little tiny underdeveloped head and my average-sized cranium, which I might add survived two seasons of brutal ACC lacrosse, there was no question of the outcome. He fell back with a thud, and his legs went limp; I rolled to the side, slightly stunned, breathing hard, but still conscious, looking at the heap next to me. "You... ok?" I asked Kelly, struggling to sit up.

"Yeah, I'm alright... are you?" Reaching out to her, she helped me stand up, and I shook my head, taking in the mess before my feet. "He won't be down for long; grab the gun and the cell phone," I said to her, stepping away from the man. She gave me the cell phone, and I opened it up to the phone call log and walked over to the counter, scanning the last three calls and writing the numbers down on a napkin.

The phone started to vibrate; it was the first number out of the three that popped up on the viewer screen.

"We've gotta get out of here before reinforcements show up," turning around, I noticed that the man was starting to stir. "We gotta move!" I said, as the phone continued to vibrate.

I opened Kelly's condo door and looked out before grabbing the man's arms and dragging him out into the rain. Releasing my grip on the man's wrist, I looked out towards the grey car and saw another man climbing out, a gun in his hand. "Hey... Hey, we got company..." I said and kicked the man's body down the four steps onto the walkway. Kelly had the man's gun and her laptop as she closed the door. "Tell me that you have a back door in these units," I said, grabbing her.

Chapter 41

Callie was thinking that Parker should have called back by now as she stepped to the waste basket to throw away her tea bag. It was her 4th of the day, and she was feeling a little wired; hell, cutting back on the coffee didn't help much. She had cut back on high-test coffee intake because of her inability to sleep at night, and the decaf didn't work. "Crap, you can't win when it comes to your health," she thought, walking back to her desk. The phone was ringing, so Callie made a beeline straight to it. Walking past the front door, she could still see that the rain was coming down in bucket loads.

Before she could sit down and answer it, the phone stopped ringing. Sliding the cup of tea across the desk and letting out a sigh of relief, Callie sat down and started working promptly on the monthly reports again.

"What's with the phones today? Lots of hang-ups and wrong numbers," she thought. "Oh well, move on." This needed to be done before the end of the week, and she wanted to corner Parker and make him listen as she went over everything. He had a way of shimming out of the monthly progress report meeting.

She had just settled into her work, listening to some soothing David Sylvian, when the phone started ringing again. Reaching for the headset, her thoughts drifted fleetingly again to her last contact with Parker earlier in the afternoon when he had just left Frankie Forsyth's office in Portage County. Now it was a little after five, and he still hadn't called back.

He had said something about having Kelly with him and that she had something pertinent to the case, maybe, and that he would check in later.

"Hello, MRO! How can I help you?" Callie replied into the headset.

There was a pause, and then a slightly familiar voice laughed and said, "Hello, Kitten... It's been a long time, now hasn't it..."

Chapter 42

Breathing hard and pulling Kelly behind me, we headed towards the only sanctuary that I knew in the immediate area. The rain was merciless. We just needed to move undetected for the next five city blocks, which could actually be about one mile depending on where you were in the city.

I had thrown the cell phone down on the landing with the man's body and took the gun from Kelly. I dropped it in her neighbor's garbage, intending to return and grab it for the police. No telling what crimes it was used in. We were now moving fast, kicking up spray between the streets that were east and south of Kelly's condo, stopping at every open area where we could be seen, which was about four places as the streets intersected with the alleys.

"Rain, rain, rain, please go away," I thought, recalling the kids' nursery rhyme, as we stopped behind a business on one of the streets in the sixties. We were breathing hard, and my head was starting to suffer residual effects from the headbutt. Not to mention, Kelly looked like she was struggling.

"Let's take a breath, are you good with that?" I asked, wiping water from my face.

"Yes, what the hell did my brother get into?" she said, laying against me, drenched and not caring about the wetness of the ground beneath her.

"I dunno, but we are in the thick of it and stumbled onto something. It's on the USB drive."

"And you can believe they want it. We just don't know what yet."

"Let's get the hell out of here first," I said, spitting water out of my mouth.

"Yeah... okay, what's next? You got a plan, Mr. Investigator, because we need a phone and some police. That's my plan," she said, inhaling and blowing out.

"Trust me, right now. I've got a place we need to make it to. It's about five blocks away," I said, moving wet hair from her face and tucking it behind her ear.

She nodded, unsure of me and the situation. I could see a blackish bruise on the back of her neck, and her face was scratched and black under her left eye.

"You good?" I asked.

"I was wondering when you were going to ask," she said, still resting her head on me.

I smiled. She was tough. Yes, the girl was tough.

"Plan?" she questioned me.

"Five blocks... we just gotta make it five more... take 'em one at a time," I replied, looking up.

Standing up, drenched, scared, and trying to survive, we exited from behind the dry cleaners that we had taken refuge at on W. 64th St and stood peering into the traffic traveling down Detroit Rd. W. 70th St. was where we needed to be. Just five more, I thought, just five more, making it my mantra. Damn, Parker! Get it together. Water was racing off our faces. We looked at each other, and I reached out and took her hand. "Run!" I yelled. It all happened in a blur. I heard the shot and saw it hit the side of the building, splintering pieces into the air. Run. The Mercedes was approaching from the right, and two men were on foot behind us where the shot originated from. Run and we did!

Chapter 43

Crossing the street, we entered the club from the alley entrance. A band was loading in their equipment for the evening show. We walked past band members and crew; no one paid any attention to us. I grabbed Kelly's wet arm and pulled her behind me as we walked towards the front and the bar area, hoping the person I needed was in. A young bartender, whom I'd seen on my occasional visits to the Bop Club, was wiping down glasses with his head down. As we approached, he looked up suddenly with great surprise to see us. Registering who I was, he smiled.

"Hey!... Parker... How ya Doing?" I reached out my wet hand and said.

"I'm good....and how are you......Kevin, right?"

"Not bad, bro.....not bad," he replied, looking at the two dripping wet visitors standing before him.

"Got a good band tonight; you two might want to check them out. I think you would dig them."

"Cool, sounds good. Oh! Kevin, this is Kelly. Kelly, this is Kevin," I introduced them.

Bop Club is one of the premier jazz clubs in NE Ohio. It hosts a lot of national performers for concerts and after-hour impromptu jam sessions. The club is also owned by Maurice "Mo" Jackson, Tiny's little brother. I asked if he was around.

Kevin explained that he was not and that at any minute, Mo should be here, having called after procuring some new ingredients for his award-winning barbecue sauce.

The Bop Club fronts south from Lake Erie's north and west from Cleveland's downtown district. It has three large tinted windows, one facing the Detroit Rd entrance, which is south. It was in this direction that I now focused my attention.

"Shit!" Parker said quietly as two cars pulled into the parking lot, a gray Benz and a dark Audi Sedan.

Parker had not seen the Audi before, which means they had called in reinforcements. Not good.

"We've got company," Parker said as he grabbed Kelly's arm and moved towards the rear door, the one we had come in earlier.

"Kevin, do us a favor, you know who I work for... don't you?"

Looking quite confused as he responded coolly, "Yeah! you're an investigator... what's up!"

"Yes, I am!" Pointing out the window as the cars parked, I said, "Them!"

I explained quickly to him what I needed done as we moved towards the back of the club.

"Oh!..hmm..... no problem," he said, twisting up his lips after I finished explaining what needed to happen. "Follow me; if these guys are looking for you, I've got a quicker way out."

The men were entering the club as we descended the stairs into the basement storeroom. Hurrying, we followed Kevin's direction towards the far end of the room and opened the door to what looked like a closet.

Nothingness is what I would describe the darkness of the void that we stepped into; a darkness so still it was chokingly claustrophobic.

"What next?" Kelly asked, breaking the momentary silence as we stood dead still.

Feeling the slight chill in the air that greeted us in this tunnel underground, I was fumbling with the Maglite that Kevin grabbed as he directed us towards the basement stairs and our impending escape.

Feeling for the wall, I said, "Forward, my good lady, and get the hell out of here."

"Hold on," Parker said as the light beam flicked on and then off. Smacking the small red flashlight on his palm, it spat out a reluctant warm glow. A collective sigh of relief could be felt.

Starting in front of them, Parker pointed the beam of the light in that direction and then traced an arc from the ground on the right-side wall over the ceiling and down the left-side wall to the ground.

He estimated that the tunnel was about six feet wide and about seven feet in height. The floor was concrete, while the walls and ceiling were brick. Parker had heard stories of thousands of tunnels throughout the city, but he had never actually seen any. This would be his first.

Putting our trust in a tepid little flashlight, whose illumination was only a sliver of light that spilled out in sporadic convulsions, was going to be, to say the least, interesting. The air in this tunnel was dry but slightly musty. Moving forward vaguely and with deliberate hesitation, Parker figured that the length might be in the range of about forty to fifty feet to the next building.

"Parker... do you think there might be rats down here?" she asked, grabbing his wet shirt, shuffling behind.

With a worried laugh, he responded, trying to concentrate on walking and assessing the tunnel.

"I wouldn't doubt it, but... hmm... I hope not."

"You think those guys will give Kevin any problems?" she asked, moving slowly.

I could see that she was still hurting, and asked if she wanted to stop and rest for a few minutes. She said no and that it was not that bad. Covering the distance with no problems from rodents, skulls, or the flashlight, they came to another door. Kevin said that there would be a key hanging on the wall to the right of the door; no key.

"Crap, it's not there!" Parker whispered.

Kelly, who was behind me, holding on to my shirt, came around and started feeling lower on the wall.

"Shine it down here," she pointed in the direction of the lower right corner.

Shining the flashlight all around the door, the walls, and the ground still provided no key!

Before concern had a chance to set in, they heard a noise, faint at first, then growing louder as it got closer, coming from the other side of the door.

Chapter 44

The two of them, Rasur and Little John, sat in the conference room discussing the validity of the information they had gleaned from their sources pertaining to Ken's case and whether it had any significance in the case that Parker was investigating at the moment. Rasur had his head down, occasionally reaching up to mop a clump of brown-streaked black hair out of his face and rub the eraser of his pencil on his forehead. He was reading a message on his iPad and now tapping an unsharpened pencil on the table.

It was an odd set of circumstances that led to a positive ID: someone had found her ID badge at the quickie mart gas station. This was half a mile from the park entrance; the station had a bulletin board and mounted the ID on it, just in case the party that lost it returns. The board is behind the cashier's checkout. A McConnell's Mill State Park Ranger caught sight of it and, being a curious sort, took a look at it. Bridgett's picture was on it—pretty blonde, blue eyes, and the company's name right next to it in bold-ass letters. Little John had his back to him at the counter, brewing himself a cup of cranberry white tea, and said, "Ras! What does it say to you?"

"....Same on the back with the exception of the picture, but instead it had writing suggesting that if found, please place it in a U.S. Mailbox."

"It says return postage-guaranteed Sys Tech Corporation Executive Pkwy. Hudson, Ohio..." Rasur continued and looked up.

"Damn great work by the Butler County Sheriff's Department..." Little John shared, returning to sit across from him.

Blowing on his steaming cup of tea, he said, "Damn good-looking young lady."

"Hat's off to the park ranger that stopped off at that quickie mart for coffee." He said, taking a sip of tea and burning his mouth. "Ah, that's smart."

"I would say the same thing to the Quickie Mart employee that found the thing on the ground and posted it on the lost and found board," Rasur said. The printer started running, and Rasur excitedly jumped up and ran over to it.

"Ok... ok.... ok, hey man, you better look at this because we are not supposed to have this yet," he blurted out.

Grabbing the paper out of the printer, he walked back over to where Little John sat, placed the paper between them, and read. After reading the paper, they both thought Ken needed to know ASAP, Rasur thought. "Phone's a ringing ding ding paling..." Rasur sang, walking back to his desk.

"Damn, this place is humping today. Anybody have a whereabouts on Parker?" Rasur asked Ken as he walked into the room, phone to his ear.

"Just a second, Rasur. Callie has an interesting call on Line one," he replied, turning around heading towards the conference room.

Little John was looking up information on Sys Tech Corporation. Turning around in his chair, he took a sip of tea, stared at the floor, and said, "Your one-stop Global toy store; they have some serious government contracts," He puffed out.

"They are not going to want to deal with this; their corporate legal department will quash any bad publicity."

Ken came back into the room with a grim look on his face and sat on the corner of Little's desk. "Ok, got some interesting news."

There was some noise out in the waiting room; voices could be heard, and someone was coming up the steps. Turning to look, Tiny entered the room with Styles trailing. "Hey, did you find P Mac?" Ken inquired.

"Yep!" Styles replied, grinning.

"Yeah, and the case just got more interesting," Tiny nodded, holding up his hand, index finger out to suggest, "give me a minute."

He walked out of the room as everyone stared, confused, waiting for the next move in this ever-growing day of unexpected circumstances. Returning with two coffees in his hand, giving one to Styles, who was now sitting on Rasur's desk corner, Tiny explained what happened.

Chapter 45

"Where are you at... okay, stay put and do not start anything at that club," Marcella smarted.

"Did the reinforcements get there?" he asked, waiting for an answer and signaling for the bartender to refill his drink. Marcella disconnected from the call and took a long pull from his drink, thinking that he needed to call Jonas and inform him now.

"Damn! Good help is hard to find," he said aloud to himself.

Taking a deep breath and exhaling, he hit the speed dial number that corresponded to Jonas' number and rubbed his face, thinking that something had to go right with this slight inconvenience.

Sys Tech Corporation, located in Hudson, is a 73,001 square foot building with generous glass lining fronting I-90, the Ohio Turnpike, offering splendid views from most of the interior offices. The peace and tranquility of the landscaping helped to diffuse the clandestine operations going on within the complex.

Every boring asshole executive and section manager at Sys Tech sat posturing for the weekly Monday meeting. This Monday, however, a different vibe flowed within. With the three Sys Tech employee deaths leading the topics and the disappearance of another, it's been causing great concerns with the Board of Directors, the shareholders, not to mention the other employees of the company.

Senior Vice President Of Human Resources Alexcia Oliver continued in her nasally high-pitched voice. "The media circus is now starting to propel forward with an enormous amount of coverage, and our legal department recommends that no one discusses the situation externally."

"As you can imagine, the employees, all of them, are in shock with what happened over the last three days," Morales Mirarck Jr. finishes. Morales Mirarck Jr., the big cheese, the big daddy, the big kahuna, is Sys Tech's President and Chief Executive Officer.

Mirarck started Sys Tech with a group of classmates and investors twenty-some years ago; one generous investor was his father, a former US Senator from the State of Utah, Paul Mirarck. The senior Mirarck, unlike his son, is one of the military's staunchest supporters, specifically their Directed Energy Weapons (DEW) programs. The Senator introduced a bill titled the Directed Energy Weapons Systems Act while in office; he also worked on the Defense Authorization Bill, which would, in part, also give the Defense Intelligence Agency and lawmakers the right to fund a new Defense Clandestine Service (DCS) and The Intelligence, Emerging Threats and Capabilities subcommittee. Morales, like most of the 150 employees at Sys Tech, has an engineering background, having come through MIT and a master's degree from the University of Cal at Berkeley. Sys Tech lost the funding temporarily when it came to light that Senator Mirarck had an interest in the company.

Morales and the employees of Sys Tech have a great relationship, considering he spent a lot of time out of the office dealing a lot with the company's long-term strategies and values with shareholders and the board of directors. He's also a master manipulator and control freak. It's not unlike him to try to capture the attention from someone else's project and claim that it was done at his suggestion.

At the young age of fifty, just recently, he looked to be in his late thirties, standing a shade under six feet and bespectacled and well-groomed. He had recently taken to dating some of the women that worked at Sys Tech; this was not uncommon or frowned upon like so many corporations today. "Thanks, Alexcia, I just want everyone to be vigilant and take care of yourself and keep an eye out for anything out of the ordinary.

"Okay, let's get down to business, Paul, you want to start?" Morales stood and stretched and looked outside the huge windows on the fourth floor conference room. It was raining pretty good out there; at least it would keep the press away from the front doors, he hoped. For the next forty-five minutes as the meeting droned on, Jonas had anticipated they would go through the normal presentation, blah, blah, blah, and lookie here, this growth chart on perspective earnings and the future growth in the tech sector, blah, blah, blah, and this is what we can expect from our quarterly projections look, blah, blah, blah. His phone vibrated, and he looked at the number. "Oh! By the way, do you know what we develop here? Yes, that's correct: weapons for the Department Of Defense that can devastate towns, hell, cities, and countries." Looking around the room as his thoughts wandered, Jonas caught the attention of Holtz Korvach, who didn't seem to give a fat rat's ass about the hoopla. Actually, he seemed as bored as Jonas; Holtz was a hard guy to figure out, always out of the office, and travels a lot. Jonas thought that was a bit odd, but he was a VP of Security & Strategy, and he didn't worry much about business projections. Still, the guy was interesting, and Jonas felt that it would be a good idea to get some background on him. Jonas was thinking about this when his attention was forced back into sharp focus with a question from another one of the big kiss-ass flunkies, Terrence Blakey! Hell, the turd didn't even spell his name properly; he was asking Jonas if he cared to share some of his insights on the new projects that he was working on. Momentarily focusing on him with a look that bordered on hatred and pure abhorrence, Jonas regrouped and explained the finer points and the trial application of the new products that he had developed for military use. Questions were asked and answered for another fifteen or so minutes, with Jonas inviting Paul Lee to add his take on the projects.

"You are dead, my friend; you just don't know it yet," he thought, smiling, looking at Terrence and shaking hands as people filed out.

"Good work, Jonas, Paul; everyone, keep it up," Morales chimed in as the meeting concluded, and everyone was walking out. "Jr. is a pussy, and Terrence is next on my list of things to do," Jonas whispered.

"Holtz, can I have a word with you?" Morales said, looking at his phone. Jonas's phone started vibrating; looking down at it, he thought, "Shit! Here we go."

Chapter 46

The two men stood looking out the window, facing each other, a sign of mutual respect. "Holtz, do you understand the position that I am in?" Morales sighed, turning to watch cars speed by on the turnpike. "I certainly do, and I'm doing everything to rectify the situation," Holtz responded, thinking that this clusterfuck was out of control. Morales had asked Holtz, at his father the Senator's urging, to keep an eye on Jonas and Paul Lee and the S.M.A.R.T program. Evidently, word had come down the political channels that the S.M.A.R.T. program was still in line for funding. The elder Mirarck still had his hands in the pie and was orchestrating from a distance. Holtz had known this was the case from the beginning. The Senator and his cronies had their hands up to their elbows in dirt; they just knew where to wash it off and on whom. Jonas was a loose cannon, and Paul Lee, well, he was the unknown factor in this unfolding craziness. Besides, Holtz had his own agenda that needed finishing.

"Good... I don't care what you do... we just have to put a lid on it... make it go away," Morales smirked.

"Something is going down fast and soon, and it's not good for the company," he continued.

Holtz walked over to the conference table and sat down, gesturing for Morales to follow him.

"I believe you're right; it ties in with two of the deaths, maybe all." Knowing that he is right; four of the five dead did have a direct tie-in to Sys Tech and its weapons program, and two of them were his work.

"Hey, what's up with this, uh... McIntyre, Reed detective agency helping one of our employees' sisters?" Morales asked.

"Yep... It's MRO... they are, from what I understand, taking her on as a client," Holtz shrugged.

"The Authorities are still investigating, so what the hell can they do but get in the way!" Morales gestured with his hands.

"Unless she has some information that they don't have, I know MRO, and they will not take a client unless they have a good reason," Holtz replied, looking out into the office at people walking around.

"Besides, the FBI is now involved, and if this other girl that disappeared turns up dead, we've got more headaches," Holtz stood up.

"I will find out what the other two are doing and keep an eye on MRO. Anything else you need?" he asked.

"Nope, that's a tall task with all of that, thanks, Holtz, appreciate it," Morales said, patting Holtz on the back.

"Mr. Mirarck, excuse me, for interrupting," it was his personal secretary, Mrs. West, leaning in through the doorway. "Toni... what's up?" "We've got two FBI agents here that would like to have a word with you," she points downstairs.

"One O'Malley and one Froom; he's the snarky one, she's the pleasant one," she finishes.

"I better take this meeting; Toni, call Alexcia and someone from the legal affairs," Morales follows her.

"You feel like sitting in?" he asks.

Chapter 47

Grabbing Kelly and pulling her back and away from the opening, we stood in the still darkness, flashlight off, staring into the brown face of a kid. "Hello, Parker dude, Kev called me and remembered that the key wasn't there." He had the smoothness and bravado of someone twice his age.

"What, fifteen or sixteen?" I thought, pulling Kelly through the door behind me and following the kid who had already turned and was making his way through the storage room. "Follow me!" He said over his shoulder. "Thanks," I said to him, putting Kelly between him and me.

We followed him through what looked like a storage room full of furniture and up a flight of stairs to another storage area. Unlike the previous one, this one had a back door.

It was still raining outside, not as hard but steady. Looking at my watch, it had only been less than an hour since we left Kelly's condo. Turning around and pointing at the alley as he talked, "Kev said that Tiny got your message and said all is good, be at the marina, we'll swoop on ya."

"Those chumps are sitting in the parking lot, four of them... two cars, silver or grey Benz, and a blue Audi." He said, pointing at a fence. "Go there, and it will get you over to the tunnel quick as shit."

"Cool, tell Kevin thanks and thank you!" I said, moving for the door.

"Oh, yeah... almost forgot, the guy in the Benz got out and made a call on the celly."

Turning back as I opened the door, "How old are you?" I asked.

He turned up his nose and said, "None of your damn business... dude!"

We stepped out into the rain, and I could hear him say. "Sixteen!... fool!

Staying close to the building as we moved east then north from W.70th and the sanctuary of the club and its surrounding business to a residential area, all of this within three short blocks.

After weaving in and out of yards, with no interaction with pets, we reached the mouth of an alley that opened up to a hopefully busy W. 67th street. "Get back!" I yelled, pulling Kelly back behind the green waste dumpster at the intersection of the street and the alley.

I caught a fleeting glimpse of the gray Benz turning around the corner and it was headed directly down W.67th towards us. "Damn! Alright, I don't think they saw us, but I could be wrong."

I could see that Kelly was starting to tighten up, and she looked weary. Hell, I felt weary.

"Parker, what the fuck are you doing, you're over your head, my friend. Just call the police and have these guys picked up, let them handle it," I was thinking.

"But then they will keep coming back for the USB drive and what's on it, and somehow this is linked to Guy's and Laurie's death and maybe others. "Okay, you alright..." I asked.

"Yes, I'm good, just tired. I'll make it.... but..." She smiled faintly.

"But what?" I asked, looking out and worrying that any second the car would pull up to the alley entrance, and we'd be forced at gunpoint into it.

"I'm troubled by two things that you did back at the bar," she said, standing up.

"One, why didn't you have Kevin call the police, two, you had the guy's cell, and you left it with him."

I was about to answer when I heard a car door close and shoes on the wet pavement moving towards our position from the direction of W.67th. Standing, I looked from the direction we had just come from and whispered, "Push!"

We pushed the bulky green mass into the mouth of the alley and ran quickly towards a backyard that we had just come through minutes ago.

I heard the car accelerate down W.67th north in the direction of what I presumed was Breakwater Avenue and a chance to head us off.

This left two excited voices behind us racing towards the big green dumpster, poised partially in the alley and the street.

The two men dispatched with the green bulk quickly, only to find an empty alley void of anything or anyone, just the relentless patter of the droning rain.

There was no way they knew where we were headed; this had to be an anticipated attempt at boxing us off from getting to the shoreway.

We were only two hundred feet from our last location; our backs rested firmly against a one-car garage surrounded by thickly dense hedges on our right, separating the next yard from our current resting place.

A seven-foot privacy fence was all that kept the alley in front of us from opening up and spilling the two of us right into the welcoming arms of our pursuers.

I could hear two other men walking towards our position, trying to be quiet—step, stop, step, step, pause, and listen; they kept this up for about twenty feet.

Looking at the hedges and then looking at the gate that we had fled through, all that it would take is for one of them to be inquisitive and start checking the next three yards, and they would stumble right onto us. A dog started to bark from a nearby house—damn! Not good.

They were about ten feet from us and closing fast. Looking at Kelly and then looking at the hedge, I pointed at a thinning section close to the garage corner. She moved to the point quietly and quickly. I followed.

Chapter 48

Zigzagging and crouching through the remaining two yards, we had reached the stairway for the tunnel entrance to the marina. At this point, we would compromise our position and be exposed.

"Well, are you ready for this?" I asked Kelly as we crouched with our backs against a small retaining wall, hidden from the view of the street.

She nodded, breathing hard and spitting out water. We had backtracked one block from the way we had initially come, missing the Benz and the two guys on foot as well.

Using my fingers to provide a silent countdown from five, I signaled.

"One!" Kelly sprang up with me right in step behind her. We ran for the stairs, turning around and looking behind us. To our dismay, forty feet down Caruso Dr. and closing fast, two men darted from the alley onto W.67th heading north towards Breakwater Ave and us.

Unfortunately, we had come out right damn smack in front of them. We still had some distance between the two, but that was slowly evaporating like hot water in a steam press. I could hear low voices and the quick footfall of the men running down the street. Turning, we jetted.

Kelly sprang and I tripped up onto the curb that protruded above the path leading down to the Edgewater Beach tunnels. Running and jumping down the short flight of stairs, we could hear the men behind us; they were gaining on us quickly now. They had not figured out which direction we had gone in; it would only take them a few minutes to figure it out. But those were minutes that we could and would use to our advantage. I ventured a look back as we cleared the tunnel, only to find one of the men giving chase out of the tunnel across the grassy area before the shoreway. He won't shoot at us out in the open, I believed, and true to this notation, he did not. But damn, he was fast.

Chapter 49

"Damn...Damn... Damn it to hell," Ken muttered as he brushed a hand through his hair, contemplating his next move. He had just gotten off the phone and was about to call it a day, but he knew that calling it a day would not take his mind off it. The Bridgett Carlson missing person case had taken a horrific and unfortunate turn for the worst. Staring out at an empty spot on the wall, he grappled with the ill and sickening vision of the crime as it played out in his mind. An informant at the coroner's office had shared that a body was identified that morning, and based on the info, it was a 24-year-old woman. Bridgett was twenty-four and missing, and now dead; this same missing twenty-four-year-old woman he was searching for was now in the morgue. Well, he sat and thought, and thought some more, before reaching for the phone. Damn case was over before it started.

"Ken, as I told your pain in the ass partner, it's an active investigation," Sheriff Frank Forsyth blasted through the phone's speaker.

"It does not matter if I like you, Ken. The law is the law, and I am a law officer. I will follow the procedures, which in my book is the law! Let's get together and fish for some crappie soon," Frank continued. "Ken, figured I'd get that in before I get pissed and hang up."

Ken was trying to stay focused on Frank's words but also trying to catch parts of the other conversation.

Frank was rambling, and Ken had just listened to a ten-minute tirade from the Sheriff of Portage County about Parker's inability to work kindly with other law enforcement communities. All that Ken had asked for was some confirmation on facts pertaining to the case. But damn! Frank wouldn't give in, and Ken had gathered some solid intel, though, of course, he hadn't shared with the sheriff what he already knew.

Then Frankie let it slip out that there was a joint task force working on this crime, including McConnell's Mills State Park Rangers, Butler County, Pennsylvania, and Portage County Sheriff's Departments.

Since the victim was from Ohio but was found in Pennsylvania, it made sense, so it was nothing groundbreaking.

He was still listening in on the other conversation when he heard someone in the other room say, "FBI."

Not thinking, he blurted out, "FBI...."

The Sheriff stopped mid-ramble and said, "How?......in the hell did you know about them being involved?"

"Aawh! got something.....maybe," Ken thought, not answering Frank's question.

"Hey Frankie, did you see Parker this morning? I'm still waiting for him to return," Ken asked, still listening to the other conversation.

"Yes, I saw him this morning before I attempted to go fishing. You know he brought me bad juju," Frank said.

"You'd be better off if he didn't show up, probably wouldn't have as many crazy cases," he rambled.

"Maybe if he didn't show up, I'd get the boat unloaded, drop a line in the water, and fish for an hour."

"No, he shows up, I get the boat unloaded, in the water, and it rains. Bad juju," he finishes, then he's off the phone, citing another important call coming in.

Ken thought he needed to inform Parker about the updates in this case, but he wasn't answering his phone, and that was unlike him.

Chapter 50

"Trust me, they are coming, we've got to move," I said, directing her forward and deeper into the cover of the marina. We entered through the south gate on the side facing the shoreway and gilded apprehensively past the office building. My hope was to lose them in the marina and then double back over to the park; that's where Tiny will look first.

It's amazing that no one was stirring within the confines of the marina. Usually, someone was out working, regardless of the weather. But damn, not today when you needed someone. We walked quickly west towards the northern right corner of the facility, and I hoped that would work to our advantage.

This would put us on a direct course for the lake and a quick exit out the west gate, directly in line for the parking lot and a fast extraction with no one in the marina getting shot. I could hear a not-too-distant horn blaring from a car towards the front gates. This told me that one or more of the men had crossed the shoreway from where we did and were closing... fast.

Kelly was now struggling. "We've got to move a little more quickly," I said. She squeezed my hand and started a half-hearted jog. "Let's do this!" she said, pepping up.

When the first man came into sight, I had just about enough time to stash Kelly between a 29-foot Wellcraft Coastal that was up on a stand for repairs.

We had made it down the drive past the refuel dock and the loading crane and were about 40 feet from the gate that separated the marina into a repair section and storage area. At this point on the marina road, it snakes to the right naturally because of the junk piled up on both sides. The road here narrows and then widens as it pushes to the right. A thinning scrap pile lazily protruded out past the right, and the green area widened before the gate, arcing the road back to the left.

The boat was on the left side between two other boats, which didn't leave much room. But because of the contour of the road and boats and other obstacles sticking out, this could help or be a potential problem.

Across from the boats was a green area that was on the lake side, cluttered with all kinds of scrap.

In this green area, a three two-level boat storage rack set between two buildings surrounded by trees provided some coverage. The best part was that it had boats on it.

"Slowly work your way towards the gate right there, using the fence and wait for me," I said quickly, looking at the approaching men. "If by chance, which will not happen, I get held up, pull the fence up and slide under..." "But... What... if..." She tried incredulously to object to what I was suggesting. I didn't hear.

I pushed her between the boats, not seeing the men approaching yet, but fully anticipating that they were carefully and hurriedly checking between all the boats as they made their way towards us.

"Trust me... run to the road when you clear. Tiny will be there, I hope..." I said, turning.

Moving across the narrow band of road towards the lake and its sea of scrape boats and other junk, I could see the storage rack was located between a taller outbuilding and a lower garage with trees on both sides of the building. This would work nicely, I thought, as I quickly climbed up the storage rack housing... three boats? Hmm? This was even better. The storage unit was deeper, actually two units placed side by side with the tree cover extending behind, providing some depth coverage.

The rain started picking up again as I climbed to the upper level and slid along the wet lateral metal supports. Rain was slowing my maneuverability down to a clumsy shuffle.

Positioning myself between the middle and last storage units, front to tail of the outermost two boats, I had just settled when the first thug appeared around the point of the scrap pile.

As he moved towards the opening around the scrap point, he stopped abruptly and stared hard and up into the storage racks. His arm was down by his side, and there was no mistaking the black object comfortably nestled in his hand. Training his eyes straight ahead again momentarily, his visual sweep quickly threaded the area where I placed Kelly, again pausing.

Left foot slide, right foot slide, left foot slide, right foot slip... "Shit...." I mumbled.

The man, who was about medium height with a slight build, turned quickly, throwing his body around and hiding the gun behind his back. There were voices coming from the direction that he had come from, and they were getting louder. Turning back around, he moved over towards the racks, training his sights on the lower rack that does not have a boat in it. If he gets closer and looks up, he will have a good shot at me. I have one chance with the rain picking up intensely. I slid quietly and quickly to my left towards him. Don't slip again, Parker, don't slip... Quickly, he whirled to his left, raising the gun and started to move across the road. Too late, stepping and half pushing, I exploded off the front railing, dropping

one hundred and ninety pounds of dead weight onto one hundred and fifty pounds, not even close, no contest... The unsuspecting thug didn't even know what hit him. I landed on his upper back and head because of the angle that he was turning as he moved across the road. I tried to regroup quickly before the other thug arrived. I was laying on my side across the guy's shoulders in the grassy area right next to the road, having bounced off him and whacking the side of my face on the muddy grassy area that I came to rest in. My jaw hurt like hell.

Getting up quickly, I looked back and saw a crumpled heap of arms and legs splayed out. Looking around the body, I did not see the gun at first. Turning to run towards the fence and Kelly, I saw the tip of the silencer sticking out from under his leg.

Lifting up his leg, I half-heartedly kicked and the gun flipped partly under the boat rack.

Standing still and listening, I could not hear anything. Then the cell phone in his pocket started vibrating, and I heard and felt the air molecules parting and something whizzing by me. Running, I didn't see where the shots came from, I just ducked and ran for the cover of the trees and the porta-john next to the storage racks. Waiting for a minute, I looked out and saw nothing back towards the road; the crumpled body was not moving, but I could still hear voices. Wedging myself out from around the garage, I took off on a dead run towards two boats up on stands next to the gate and the corner of the fence.

"Kelly, it's me...where are you at?" I whispered, wiping wet hands down my face.

Nothing, just the beating rain. I could not even hear the voices anymore. That must mean the other shooter might be moving in on this position after he gets his partner. I called out again in a whispered tone with the utmost urgency starting to creep in. I called out once more. "Kelly!... Kelly!" Nothing, just rain. I had reached the farthest corner that separated the two parts of the marina gate, which was locked.

"Well shit, I better work back down the fence line and find her," turning and sliding down behind a cabin cruiser. "Parker..." She whispered and touched my back.

Whirling around, half scared out of my mind, I grabbed and hugged her tightly. "Let's go!" I grabbed her.

Reaching down on both sides of the pole, I pulled the fence up 2 feet from the ground, allowing her to shimmy on her back through. Bending down, Kelly grabbed the fence from the opposite direction and started pulling. "Parker! Look..." She pointed as I turned around.

A dark figure came out of nowhere and jumped on me, landing a blow to my stomach, knocking the wind out of me and causing me to roll over into the protective position. Balled up hands over my head, this was all that I could do to protect myself from the kicks to my back, my head, my side, all with a frenzy of animalistic fury.

My assailant then bent down to punch me, and it was at this moment that Kelly poked a stick through the fence, catching him right on the side of the face between the eye and his nose, causing him to stagger backward, screaming in agony. His hands were clutching his face. It was at this moment that I had my chance, no matter how much I hurt. Standing as fast as possible, I launched a kick right into his groin, sending him flailing backward into the hull of the cabin cruisers. His head hit with a sickening thud; down he went.

"What's next?" She asked, pulling the fence up quickly with some effort.

"Thanks," I said, sliding under and standing and hugging her. Sirens could be heard in the background approaching as I saw a familiar vehicle rounding the corner of the parking lot. I grabbed her arm and ran towards it.

Chapter 51

"Hey!.....Hey!......Hey! Sir, may I help you?" asked the man dressed in a flower shirt and garish-looking cargo shorts, hustling towards Johnny D. He was as tall as he was round, with a fleshy face and a balding dome. With his pink umbrella in hand, he resembled a sea world walrus.

Turning around and sliding the gun into the back of his pants and covering it with his shirt, Johnny D turned on his megawatt smile and charm. Approaching the man in a non-threatening manner, he threw his hand up in a mock gesture as if to say, "Hey, yes, there you are. I was looking for you." Bullshit! This again had the potential to get out of control.

He was formulating a plan and hoping that Slim Jenkins, the guy Marcella had sent over to replace dumbass Carl, didn't walk back around that wall of junk, or worse, start firing on the man and the woman.

"Hey, my friend, how are you on this wet day?" he said quickly.

"Could you help me? I'm looking for my dog. His name is Cujo," he said, smiling, wondering if the lump might get his wry sense of humor.

"No, I have not seen your dog. What kind of dog is it?" the man answered, looking quite wet and taken aback by the name.

Looking around just in case he had trouble with the guy and he'd have to pop him on the head, Doc said, "A border collie..." thinking that he didn't have time for this crap.

"Well, sir, this is a private area for the marina. It's only for repairs and storage of members. Are you one?"

"What was that sound?...Did you hear that?" the Walrus asked, looking towards the area in the back.

Oh fuck! Doc thought. They are firing. Thank god they have silencers on the guns. Cool at all times, he directed the conversation back to the dog. "I didn't hear anything, or it might be my dog. You know, Cujo."

Turning around, Doc thought that he heard a commotion going on back around that point where the scrap was piled up and the road turned back to the right.

"Well, are you a member, sir?" the man asked again.

"Yes... of course I am...why in the hell would I be out here chasing my Cujo..." Doc answered, thinking, I'm going to shoot this rotund piece of crap in about two seconds.

"Do you have your membership card with you?" he asked, holding the umbrella back and pushing a couple of strands of what was left of his hair out of his eyes and sticking out his hand for the card.

"Aw, goodness, I do not have it with me. Why don't you go to the office and look up Mr. Paul Jensen?" He said this trying to look put out and then recited a fake address.

"Fine! Stay right here! And why would you name a dog after that monster...HUH?" He pivoted and made the walk back to the office. He got it. shit, the man's not as dense as he looks, Doc thought, turning up his lips.

"Bud, you don't know how close you came to getting shot in the ass!" Doc replied quietly with the rain falling off his head and down his face. He turned around, pulled out the gun, and headed towards the point in the road where he heard the noise.

As he rounded the corner, he saw what he had heard. Parker was bent over the crumpled body of Slim and kicking his gun under the boat storage racks. Doc could hear sirens, and now the girl had dropped a stick and was pulling the fence up, helping Parker slide through. Marcella will not like this, he thought, turning and walking away just as the man returned.

"I cannot find your card," he snarked.

"My bad, wrong place." He grinned and hit the man with the butt of the gun across the head.

"Your lucky day, dude." He smiled and walked away.

Chapter 52

The neighbors milled around with concerned anticipation as the police questioned Kelly and took reports about the home intrusion. I caught Tiny and Styles up on the events that had taken place over the last few hours; he, in turn, filled me in on the situation back at the offices.

Tiny explained to me that he received the message from Kevin and they attempted to call my cell, but it kept going to voicemail, so they headed over to the address I had left with Kevin. He then decided to use the phone tracker and realized the phone was inside Kelly's place. At that point, Styles said Kevin's message mentioned that I was headed to the marina.

"Well, P Man! What's your next move?" Tiny questioned, as if he was afraid of the answer.

The first thing I thought, as I tried to listen in on the conversation that Kelly and the officer were having, was that she would not be safe here tonight. I needed to get some dry clothes on and some food in me. The officer questioned me after Kelly, and I kept it brief. I just told him what we had agreed on, just the bare facts. Officer Pedro Garcia and his partner concluded the investigation by telling us that we might have to go downtown for more questioning, but if that happens, we will be notified.

On his way out the door, his partner, who had not said much, turned and asked if we had seen or heard any gunfire down at the marina.

"Wow! NO! You think our guys here might be involved?" I asked.

"No, just wondering," he said. "We got a call on the radio that some cars are responding to a disturbance down there."

Kelly's condo door sustained minimal damage, so securing the place would not be a major problem.

Tiny and Styles went outside with the police officers, chatting about people they knew at the 4th District Precinct. Tiny had mentioned to me earlier that a look around was in order before we left.

This gave me time to inform Kelly that she was staying with me until we sort this out, like it or not!

Following Tiny and Styles back to I-90 West, I was trying to process the events that had unfolded since this morning at the sheriff's office. I called Ken at the office, and he brought me up to speed on the cases and how they seemed to be connected. Ken ended the call when he received an important message and said that he would get back to me this evening. Kelly was quiet, probably wondering what she had gotten herself into with this guy that she really doesn't know.

I pretty much told her that I was going to carry her out of her place and that she could not stay, due to the fact that whoever attacked us was playing very serious ball here, so pack up some things.

Battered and bruised, Kelly decided that she did not want to go to the emergency room to get her head checked after a paramedic on the scene recommended rest and confirmed that she didn't show signs of being concussed. I believe when I refreshed her memory about the guy attacking her and the gunshots, it sealed the deal. Breaking my train of thought, she asked, "What's next?" The rain had subsided, and I adjusted the speed of the windshield wipers, wondering the same thing.

"Dunno," I replied, looking to my left and changing lanes before checking my rearview mirror. "First, we need to get some food and dry clothes," I said. "Then we can think this through."

"Tiny said that the office had some info there for us." Smiling, she said, "Okay, sounds good."

We pulled into my garage and were getting out of the car when I noticed my neighbor across the street hurriedly striding over. Henry Bassett was a retired Army Colonel and liked to consider himself the self-appointed guardian of the neighborhood. I liked him; he was sharp and had an astute eye for detail.

"Parker, how are you doing? Thought you should know an automobile was parked down from your place." He said this in one quick, rhythmic cadence. "How are you doing, little lady?" he said to Kelly.

"I hope that you're not in some kinda trouble that you are involving us in, like on the TV shows I watch."

Smiling, I said, "No, Sir. What kind of vehicle?" Kelly smiled too and chimed in, "Hello!"

"Government, maybe. Black SUV!" he asserted.

"Did you see the driver or license plate?" I asked, retrieving Kelly's bag.

"That would be a double negative—dark glass and plate cover, glare didn't allow it."

"...but if they return, I will," he finished.

I thanked him and reassured him that it was nothing and that I was not bringing an element to the neighborhood that he should be concerned about.

Chapter 53

Doc explained to a severely pissed-off Marcella as best he could, but it didn't matter.

"I had one sit on the girl's place, and I got the big dumb asshole out of there…"

"…Parker clubbed him with a laptop. Apparently, it had the photos on it," Doc finished.

"…And they returned with a big-ass black guy and a small white guy. Cops were there... yeah!"

He paused to listen to the voice on the other end of the phone, shuffling uncomfortably, standing out in the open at urgent care.

"He's all right, just a broken little nose, and he wants to kill Parker... The marina shit is another matter," he said, listening.

"Yeah... I cleaned up what I could. The girl fucked up Slim's eye... he'll survive and won't lose it. Jimbo was clocked hard."

"Got them out of there just as the police arrived, so what's next?" Doc, his most reliable guy, was asking. Marcella was going to close ranks and take care of this problem quickly. He sent two guys over to watch Parker's house earlier, and now he needed results fast.

"Stay loose, and I will get back to you," Marcella told Doc. "I don't want to have an outcome like this again, or it's someone's ass."

He snarled, disconnected, and figured now was as good a time as any to call Jonas.

Jonas was enraged and started taking his displeasure out on the speed bag in the workout room of his luxury home overlooking the Portage Lakes south of Akron. The intensity at which he hit the bag made it a wonder the straps on the mount didn't break loose.

His phone rang, and he ignored it. It rang again… and again… and again. He seemed oblivious to the incessant ringing. Marcella had just informed him of his inability to get the package from Kelly's place and that he would try again this evening. Jonas was not in the mood for Marcella's failure, not to mention the FBI showing up at the office today, questioning Morales. And what the hell was Holtz doing in there? That alone bothered him.

The business contacts wanted a delivery date for the S.M.A.R.T., and it was within the next couple of days. These were powerful people who got what they wanted and were not used to delays.

It had to be done; you do not fuck with these people after taking their money. The consequences would be grave. The phone had stopped ringing. Grabbing a towel, he wiped the sweat from his face and neck.

Walking over to the table where he had placed the phone, Jonas looked at the number and thought... shit! Make the call.

Chapter 54

"What's his name? And how did he come upon this..." Parker was asking excitedly.

The knot in his stomach had tightened so much that he felt like breathing would cause him to explode.

After settling Kelly into the guest room, they had worked on trying to identify the people in the picture from her brother's micro drive.

"Ok, ok, yeah, alright. I'm going to contact him... yeah, got it. Whip Jordan... I'll touch base."

"Any word from the police on the men that attacked us?"

Listening to the voice on the other end, Parker frowned and replied, tapping the pencil on his knee.

"I know it's not over. They were sent by someone."

Kelly was sitting on the couch with a glass of wine and her new bestie's head in her lap, listening curiously. Parker seemed supercharged after receiving the call from Ken. If they could only ID the other faces on the micro drive and the men who were chasing them, then they might be able to relax a little. But right now, things were not as they should be, and he was worried. They had to get out of town, and this might be what was needed—a short-term answer for an increasingly bad situation.

Disconnecting from the call, Parker picked up his drink, still holding the phone with the other hand, and said, "Whew! We might have that break needed to tie the cases together and then some."

Sitting down next to Kelly, he proceeded to explain the phone call from Ken and what was on his mind for the next move. A Utah District Ranger named Whip Jordan, who oversees a large area of Ashley National Forest, which includes the Flaming Gorge Reservoir district on the Utah side, is currently investigating a double murder. "Guess what case, Rebecca Richmond, Laurie Rice's friend."

"Oh damn! It continues to get crazier by the second. What did my brother get involved in?" she asked.

Standing and thinking about this, Parker went to check on the red pepper and spinach pesto pizza in the oven. Opening the oven and looking, he deemed the pizza ready.

"Let's eat! The pizza's ready, and that salad you made looks fantastic."

"Have you ever heard of using a timer? That really expensive oven has one, you know," Kelly said as she got up to refill her wine glass and get a slice of pizza. They ate and discussed the current developments in the case.

"So, while out on the scene Saturday morning," Parker continued, "Whip came across a wallet with a driver's license, credit cards, and various receipts." Pausing, he said, "It was my uncle's wallet."

"Big Jim's wallet. From the look of it and how it was discovered, it's been there for a long time."

Taking a drink from his glass, he stood and walked over to the bookcase, where a host of pictures were on the shelf. Picking up one with two young boys and a young girl holding fishing rods, three adult males were standing behind them. All were smiling, standing in a river between what looked to be huge mountains around them.

"Brother Chase, Callie, Uncle Jim, Cyrus, and Wallace McHenry, a close family friend," he pointed out.

"We were standing in the Green River in Wyoming. Good times," he reminisced.

"Ok, what does this have to do with the events of today?" Kelly asked, sipping her wine and pushing the laptop away.

"Thanks, lost in thought anyway... well, it does and it doesn't... maybe," he said, explaining his idea about the double murder and how it could relate to their case, along with the bonus of his uncle's wallet being found in the area where he disappeared years ago.

"Parker, we need to talk to this Whip. Are you going to call him?"

"He's three or four hours behind us, so you should be able to reach him," she pushed.

Parker retrieved his phone and said, "Better... we are going to see him."

"After the events today, some distance and time away might help us figure this crap out," he said.

Chapter 55

The two men watched as Parker loaded two small overnight bags into the back of the Cayenne, closing the hatch door and walking around to the rear of the house to let the dog in from doing his business. They had been there yesterday and were going to attempt to break in but noticed the high-tech security system that his house and the other homes in the development employed. Driving around the area, waiting for the guy to come home, was becoming a pain, and the two wanted to just take care of the business they were hired to do: retrieve the package and get the hell out.

But now there was a hitch. The girl had come back with him, so now there were two problems, and they had seen what was in the package. They had returned again last night and watched through the window as they viewed the contents of the micro drive. The dude received a phone call just as the dog sensed they were there and walked over to the window, so they beat feet back to the car, causing other neighborhood dogs to bark. They were lucky no one saw them cutting through the yards.

"Did you hear the Parker dude mention Utah twice in that call he received?" the shorter one asked.

"Yeah, he mentioned Salt Lake and Flaming Gorge... So what?" the bespectacled man answered.

"Better let the man know," the short one suggested. So now, seated in a car that smelled of fast food and cheap cologne, fighting the confines of a flatulent coffin, their demeanor had heightened to an agitated state, bordering on impulsive and irrational.

It was starting out as another sticky day. They had alternated turning the air conditioner on and off during the duration of the stakeout. Thank God the rain had stopped.

"Dude, look!" the shorter one tapped his partner on the shoulder.

"Yeah, I can see... shoot him." Smiling, the tall bespectacled man suggested and started laughing.

"Can't do that... too much noise... and the cleanup... mmmbitch man... bitch," the short one said, looking to the right and behind him. Since he was driving, no surprises were needed, like someone sneaking up on him.

"Looks like they are off on a trip... which means the airport," the short one said.

"Or they could drive," responded the tall one.

"Either way, they can't make that trip." They smiled, and a text was sent to Jonas.

Parker had booked two seats on a 6:05 flight to Salt Lake City. It was now 4:00, and he hadn't slept much last night. He figured it was due to being on edge from the previous day's activities and the soreness of his body. He refused to believe that it could be from having a beautiful and attractive woman sleeping in his guest room, maybe. They exited Rt 480, headed towards CLE Airport, and took the turnoff to the parking area for departing flights. Parker had been checking for a tail since they had left his house and didn't stop now. Taking the ticket and turning into the first available spot, which was at the end of the row, Parker tapped Kelly on the shoulder, who had been sleeping since they had left the house.

"Hey, sleepyhead..." he said gently, looking up into the rearview mirror as car lights passed by them.

"Wow! That was quick, felt like I just dozed off," she said, stretching her arms out and scratching her head, smiling. "Did you get much sleep last night?" she asked, unsnapping her seatbelt.

"No thanks to you," I replied.

She looked good. Her hair was pulled back into a ponytail, and it was hard to concentrate with her cargo shorts riding high, exposing muscular thighs and those long legs.

"What! Me?" she retorted, climbing out and walking towards the rear. This brought my attention back.

I followed and was opening the hatch when I felt a punch to my lower left back, doubling over and falling forward against the back bumper, narrowly missing the hatch door with my head. As the pain was spiraling, a raspy low voice broke the nanosecond of chaos, telling Kelly not to scream or she would quickly die.

"Mr. Parker, dude, you have something that my employer wants..."

"...and before you deny, think about your girlfriend."

"Ok... yes," I replied, turning to look for Kelly's location. She was standing to my right with a terrified look on her face, and a skinny long arm encircling and squeezing her left breast. I was enraged. The man behind me must have sensed my feelings because he reached up and grabbed the hatch and slammed it down on me as I heard Kelly moan from the pain being inflicted.

"Ok, it's yours," I said as I went down again onto the luggage in the trunk.

"Then let's get it on. I've got something special planned for you and this hot little number here." The other man had not spoken yet and seemed content holding onto Kelly's breast in a vise-like death grip.

"It's in my bag. You can get it out."

He was standing directly behind me, close enough that I could not move out from the bent-over position that I was currently in. I had to make this count and move fast. His hands were still on the hatch. I looked at Kelly, caught her eye, and mule-kicked the muthafucker straight in his nuts.

The power and sudden snap sent his ass stumbling backward. The man holding Kelly tried to throw her to the side, but she used the sudden explosion in movement to push backward, slamming her head into the man's chin and both of them into a car parked next to them. As this was happening, I rolled out from under the hatch, clutching my monopod. All I needed was two strides, and I reached the man holding Kelly. He was clumsily struggling to get up. I hit him with a sickening thud, and he went limp, falling sideways to the ground, his glasses landing broken by his side. Kelly was leaning against the SUV, breathing hard. Turning, I saw the other man, shorter in build, running towards me, reaching into his jacket pocket. I ran toward him and launched myself. We collided with the impact of two football players on the field.

Chapter 56

But I sincerely believe she doesn't know," he said, explaining this to Jonas as they sat, trying to do damage control of the now ever-expanding and unrelated incidents coming to light.

"For one thing, the authorities' investigation is going nowhere," Paul Lee insisted, smiling devilishly.

Thinking about this for a minute, stroking his hand through his already tousled hair, Jonas turned around in his chair and contemplated this current development in an already mushrooming problem.

The FBI was asking questions, specifically Cafren O'Malley, the agent in charge, and this Parker dude and a dead engineer's sister who has the micro drive with the damaging photos of him on it, along with a bunch of dead people. Rubbing his chin thoughtfully, he replied, "This means then, hmm, they don't know about the properties yet, I presume."

"Or us!" Paul Lee said, holding his hands against his lips, simulating a prayer posture.

"Boom! Very good, then we stay on task. The deal has got to go down; we have too much at stake," Jonas continued, smiling.

"Yes, one hundred million reasons, and we need to find that Parker dude and his girl pal," Paul Lee frowned.

"He's causing us great concern. Any ideas?"

"Absolutely! Yes, since you asked. Marcella has informed me, both of them are on their way to Utah."

"Utah! Utah! What the fuck for?" Paul stood up, seriously surprised.

"Jonas! Do you know what's in the neighboring state of Wyoming?"

"Yes, I do," he said, staring at Paul Lee and then smiling. "Hoo hoo yes, and it might work to our advantage... ok, maybe."

Jonas stood and now was pacing around the office. Shit, this was getting exciting.

Sitting back down, he had an idea and, reaching across the big spacious oak desk that separated him from Paul Lee, he grabbed his phone and said, "We need to get Marcella's ass out there... that guy's a sociopath, he likes to kill... and have him call his friend."

"Oh boy, that guy's scary..." Paul Lee said carefully.

"Are you sure about this? He screwed up the home invasion."

"...and the airport thing and the other girl thing... shit! Jonas, I'm losing count."

"Yep, he did, and we need to fly out... call and see if the jet is available," Jonas paced around the office.

"Shit!... I'm feeling it, Jonas," Paul smiled, realizing what Jonas was planning.

"Yes, my boy, we are going to make the exchange out in Wyoming and wrap the whole thing up out there." Jonas rubbed his hands together.

"We will use the Green River facilities to stage from and set the meet and exchange up at a secluded area around there. There's a lot of isolated wilderness and cover for the exchange to go down," Jonas explained his thinking to Paul Lee, who was in total agreement. This could work, they thought.

"But what about Marcella and his group?" Paul asked.

Shrugging his shoulders and holding his hands in the air, Jonas replied, "Paul, the guy likes to kill, what's wrong with that?"

"If you had the balls to do it, you would too. It's like sex; once you do it, you want to do it some more." He laughed. "Now listen to this," he continued, explaining more of his ideas.

"He'll arrange for his people to get there if he hasn't already. I'll have him scout a location for the exchange and whatnot... you good with this, Paul?"

"This should be fun, man. Loosen up, we are rich, bitch, and it will all be over soon," Jonas continued.

Looking down at his watch, Jonas realized that they needed to hurry to get things done. Getting up and walking around the desk, he asked Paul Lee if he had seen Mirarck or Holtz.

"Would not surprise me if they were off somewhere doing his old man's dirty work," Paul Lee responded, laughing.

"Surprise is as surprise does!" Jonas laughed.

Chapter 57

"Southwest Airlines flight 2964 for Salt Lake City will be boarding at gate 17," the speaker boomed.

It felt like the announcer was right in my ear. I guess the residual effects from the confrontations were starting to catch up to me—I hurt. Shit! My head, my back, my body was hurting. Squinting and looking into the bathroom mirror, I could see dark bags under my eyes. I felt worse than the image staring back at me in the mirror. A scratch on my cheek and the back of my hand—not bad, I thought, turning and dropping a paper towel in the wastebasket and noticing someone sitting quietly in a stall. I paused, wondering, shook my head, and walked out, cautiously aware, looking behind me.

Kelly placed a soft, weary hand on my temple and kissed my forehead, rubbing my hair. "Are you going to be alright?" she asked, smiling.

It was a question as much as a statement of affirmation, and it felt nice.

"Yeah... how are you feeling?" I asked, pointing at her.

"These..." she said, grabbing her breast. "The left is sore and bruised, the right not so much," she paused. "The bastard gripped it like he wanted to rip it off, and the way he was breathing... grinding against me..."

"What's up with these guys and breast grabbing?" she asked. I just shrugged and smiled.

"I'm going to have you massage them," she said slyly, smiling. I just kept smiling back, feeling an ever-growing anticipation to do just that.

"Yeah... these people are wearing me," I said, reaching in my jacket for our boarding passes. "Hopefully, Tiny found what he was looking for and called the police and explained." She expelled a breath and stopped. Turning, she grabbed my arm and said, looking up at me, "You scared me when you crashed into the man."

"How bad do you think they are?" Kelly asked?

My answer was straight to the point, "I don't care!

"Kelly, they had guns, and we were dead in their eyes."

"I'm sorry, but I value our lives and not theirs... the police will figure it out with Tiny's input."

I had made a call to Tiny and the airport police right after the confrontation, not leaving my name with them—an anonymous caller.

"The FBI are on the case and want to have a sit-down," I said to her, relaying what Tiny had informed me of as she continued to walk ahead of me. Damn, what an attractive sight she was. She casually smirked, adjusted her carry-on bag, and looked around to see if we were being followed. Those guys are still on the lookout for us, and I am sure that the FBI can't be too far behind them and us. Reaching down, I checked my cargo pocket for the iPhone that I took from one of the hired thugs. I needed to slip it into a bag going to another destination. He will not be needing one in this lifetime. It was now 5:40 am, and the flight would be departing CLE Airport in 20 minutes, landing in Salt Lake City at around 10:10 am mountain time.

We boarded without any problems and sat in the back of business class. This would afford us a first-hand look at everyone that came on after us. The flight was full, and we didn't notice anyone paying attention to us, although there were a couple of gentlemen that did look quite familiar.

But hey, it's a big city, and some of the people on the flight I might have seen in day-to-day life in the big city of Cleveland. I had told Kelly back at the house about a close family friend who lived in Utah that I had contacted last night when she was sleeping. He would be expecting us, and from there, we would be going to Flaming Gorge.

Kelly slept for a good portion of the flight, leaning on me as I navigated around on the laptop. It felt good, considering the non-stop running that we've been doing since I took this case.

I had just started to doze as our flight started its descent. "What time is it?" she asked, lifting her head off my shoulder and rubbing her eyes. Damn, she smelled good, I thought, answering, "9:50, we are ahead of schedule." Looking out the window, I could see the mountainous border of the Wasatch Range to the east, running the length of the Salt Lake City metropolitan area and points south to Provo and Utah Lake. The view was breathtaking as we circled to line up for our landing, and the Great Salt Lake came into view with Antelope Island, its large and most constant feature.

Ohhhh, pain! shot through my body as I adjusted myself in the seat. Crap! It was hard to pick one spot that didn't hurt. The fasten your seat belt sign came on, and the flight attendants were walking up and down the aisle, checking on the passengers when I caught a glimpse of someone familiar. Kelly was straightening up, glancing out the window, and wasn't paying attention.

Chapter 58

Kelly let Parker deal with the rental car agent, instead opting to sit and reflect on the last five days and how the current situation had affected her, her brother, and the others who died unnecessarily. She was deep in thought when Parker asked her if she had noticed the man standing by the baggage carousel, watching them.

"I'm sorry... huh, what man?" she said, standing and looking inquisitively in that direction.

Parker pointed, but the man was gone.

"Right there when I was signing for the car, I turned to check on you and saw him."

"He wasn't being discreet about it," he said, with concern on his face.

Shaking his head and biting his lower lip in thought, Parker grabbed their bags and headed for a shuttle, looking around as they exited the terminal. The late summer weather was comfortable in the high 80s with a mild breeze. They loaded the bags into the back of a Jeep Grand Cherokee and set out 175 miles east to the town of Vernal. Kelly had never been to Utah, so she was very impressed with the scenery as they drove east on I-80 from SLC airport towards downtown SLC and the beautiful and majestic Wasatch Mountains.

I explained as we merged onto I-15 and then back onto I-80 East, south of the capital city, that this region is called the Wasatch Front, which extends from Ogden and Layton in the north down to West Valley City and Provo in the south. SLC sits right in the middle. We started our climb up into the mountains, following I-80's winding and breathtaking scenic views headed towards Park City. The higher we climbed, I could feel my ears popping. Kelly's ears must have been too because she started rummaging around in her bag.

"Gum! Here," she smiled, unwrapping a piece and putting it in my mouth.

"Thanks," I said. We didn't speak much for the next few miles, just enjoying the views, the silence, and each other's company. Clearing Heber City, the car's Bluetooth system chimed with an incoming call. Kelly looked at the dash screen and pushed the caller's name—it was one of the calls we were waiting on.

"Son, how are you doing!"

It was Wallace McHenry.

I had texted him on the plane and informed him on what time to expect us here and some of what was going on. His response was to get out here and let's talk about it—no sense in discussing it on the phone.

"Flight was good, we are doing well," I responded.

"Good... good! Where are you kids at?" he said in his smooth baritone. I told him that we had cleared Heber City and were coming upon Strawberry Reservoir.

"Ok, your ETA should be around an hour and ten minutes... good... see ya then," he pointed out. Never one for small talk, Wallace was a man of principle and no bullshit, and God did he love his fishing. I couldn't wait to see him—it was like seeing family. Yeah, that was it—it was like seeing family. Kelly was looking at me, and I just smiled.

Chapter 59

Sweetwater County Airport was located 29 minutes east of Green River on I-80 out of Rock Springs. This was one of the dusty, godforsaken places that Jonas did not like visiting very much, but the facilities in Green River were state-of-the-art, just like the one in Lake Charles, Louisiana. It was off the beaten path, good for testing products, and there was an agenda that drove them to this location. It was also 45 miles south of Utah, killing two birds with one stone. The company's Range Rover hummed down I-80 outside of Rock Springs with Jonas, Paul Lee, Marcella, and Facilities Manager Jim Masterson, who was on his way back from Lake Charles.

It was perfect timing that Jim was on his way back and had stopped over in Hudson. Jonas was able to procure one of the jets from Burke Lake-Front and tie it into an investigative trip to Wyoming to look into the procurement of new testing equipment for a product being developed by a newly hired engineer, who would be flying back with them to Ohio. Their stay was to be no more than a couple of days. Marcella was quick on the draw to send his best man out to the airport as soon as he received the message from the two guys that staked out Parker's house.

Fools! They could not even take the flash drive from the two at the airport in Cleveland, and now it's led to all of this, a fitting twist of fate in the desert.

He thought as the car hummed down the two-lane desert road, sensing the intense desert heat clawing at the outer confines of the Range Rover's sleek white hull. Beautiful soaring mountain bluffs and foothills surrounded them. The reds, browns, and greens in the distance framed magnificent peaks jutting toward the intensely azure blue sky. It would be great if you liked it, he thought.

Beautiful country if you like the desert and rock, unlike his war-torn Baltimore neighborhood with its claustrophobic grip on those that had the misfortune of living in its inner belly.

If it wasn't for Johns Hopkins, he would have never had the chance, he thought as his phone vibrated.

Looking at the screen, he smiled at the message. "It's a beautiful day out here in God's country... aha." Marcella said, showing the cell to Paul Lee, who was in the back seat with him. The message said, "I'm following them now." Paul Lee smiled and gave him the thumbs-up sign. Jonas and Jim Masterson were engaged in conversation about the new development at Lake Charles and here in Wyoming, so he didn't see. Jim was telling Jonas about the growth around Green River and how the one hundred employees at this location worked quite a bit with robotics.

"Looks like the city has been growing since I was last here," Jonas said, looking around as Jim drove through the downtown area of Green River, and everyone looked up at Castle Rock in all its magnificence, towering up to 5,783 ft.

Turning into the parking lot, Jim informed the group that, unfortunately, he would not be there to show them the equipment, but there would be someone at the facility to help them. He had to be in Laramie by tomorrow for another meeting with the state energy commission.

Chapter 60

Tool was thinking how freaking nice this state was as he drove up the two-lane canyon road past Park City Ski Resort. He was trying to keep a four-car-length advantage behind the vehicle he was tailing—no sense in alerting them. That, my friend, had almost happened at the airport twice, he thought. Marcella was lucky that he was still available and in the area for the job; actually, this might work out perfectly, he sensed. When he received the call last night, it was easy to check out all flights leaving for SLC and get to the airport early the next morning to stake the place out. Damn, what luck— he got one of the last three seats on the same flight. Nice, he smiled.

Taking a turn too fast at Strawberry Reservoir, he had closed the distance on the tail and decided to lag further back. Tool had been to Utah a few years back on a job over toward the Nevada line in a town called Overton. That job was an in-and-out, but it's important to have resources near any prospective job and a way to accumulate the needed hardware for the task at hand. For this job, he called in one of those resources, who came through righteously.

The Vernal city limits sign had just come into view, and he could see that the Jeep Cherokee was signaling to exit at Vernal-W. Main St.

Three miles north at Vernal Regional Airport, Shooter/Holtz was in the process of putting his bags in his rental Tahoe when his phone started chiming. He had just turned it back on, not wanting anyone to track his movements. He had caught a quick flight from Flagstaff, Arizona, that morning, hoping to beat everyone's movement, and now this.

"Hey, what's going on?" he said into the phone, waiting for a response and grabbing his backpack and throwing it into the rear seat.

"I don't believe that I will be meeting up with Jonas and Paul Lee in Wyoming," Shooter/Holtz was saying, looking into the side mirror and pulling out into traffic. "Morales... yep, I will return in a couple of days from Lake Charles... yes! that's where I am," he said as he drove north out of Vernal city limits, turning onto Rt 44, headed towards Manila.

"Yes, I am sure... the Intelligence, Threats Subcommittee will still be happy," he said, slightly distracted, thinking, you mean your father, the Senator. He had a mission to complete, and it really depended on all factors working towards his final outcome. Holtz had worked too hard putting some of the final strokes on this canvas, although some of those strokes just fell into place by happenstance, and like a very attentive student, he would capitalize on them.

Chapter 61

The four men arrived from Cheyenne looking frazzled. They had just driven four hours after a morning flight from Cleveland to Denver, followed by a quick fifty-minute jump up to Cheyenne Regional Airport, and then the previously mentioned drive. The four checked into a Holiday Inn Express and were told to get some food and rest. Carl "Bang" Smitt, Slim Jenkins, Marko Blanks, and Jimmy "Doc" were the four that Marcella called up for reinforcements for the exchange with the Europeans. The deal was half the cash up front, wired to numbered accounts, and the remaining balance upon delivery and inspection. The European contingent was en route from Denver and would be arriving this evening for the completion of the agreement.

Doc opened the door to his room and looked around, feeling slightly uneasy. He'd never gone into a job waiting for someone else to provide the firepower. Marcella had reassured him that the people providing the weapons were on top of things and had arranged for a four o'clock meet. They were based out of the Denver area; it seemed like everything up here was coming out of Denver.

Hell, he figured, based on the lack of big cities and suburban towns, that made sense. This place was pretty damn desolate, like something out of a western movie, with its painted rocky buttes and deep canyons. They had driven by a big mass of mountain called Pilot

Butte, 7,949 ft huge, out in the middle of nothingness. He knew this from looking it up in the car on his iPhone. Damn! Doc thought, what if. Thank god for the cell service, he thought, throwing his bag on the bed.

The people seemed friendly though, and the country was pretty, he was thinking when his cell started to vibrate.

"What's up?" he said, pulling back the curtains and looking up at Castle Rock and thinking about climbing it if he had the time.

It was Marcella. "Hey, I see you guys made it in. Very good, we're on schedule."

"How's everyone? They need to be sharp." This was in reference to "Bang" Smitt's and Slim's run-in with Parker and Kelly the other day.

"Bang is good, slight head, nose ache, and a... Slim's eye will be fine, he's got a patch on it," Doc replied.

"Shit, can he see?" Marcella asked.

"It's fine. The girl got him in the eyelid. A few cm either way, and the dumbass would be blind." He smirked and filled him in on Marko and how they needed to keep a tight leash on the young buck. He could be worse than Bang in the jumpy department.

Marcella filled him in on the plan, which included picking up weapons at four or so with a trusted source and loosely about getting the USB drive from

Parker and Kelly, plus their support of the product and its delivery to the Europeans.

"I've got someone following them now," Marcella finished. "So hang tight for a few."

Chapter 62

Wallace's house was a wood-sided rambler ranch that sat back off the road, up on a wooded rise surrounded by beautiful trees—ponderosa, pinyon pines, Utah juniper, and quite a few white firs. It was so peaceful and serene. Driving up the dirt road, we could see Wallace and his dog Mitch, a golden retriever, walking out of the front door and standing on a wrap-around deck that traveled the length of the house. By the time we parked and got out of the car, Wallace was standing at the door, putting a huge hand out for me to shake.

"How are you, Parker? It's so good to see ya," he said, smiling. Kelly walked around the car, escorted by Mitch, who was sniffing and bumping into her leg. Turning to greet her, still smiling, Wallace stuck out his hand, and she shook it, introducing herself.

"Mitch, that's enough," he said to the dog. "Come on in, let's get out of this heat," he said, turning and walking towards the house.

Wallace is a big man, standing six feet four and two hundred and thirty pounds of muscle, still looking like the offensive tackle he was at the University of Utah, minus about sixty or so pounds.

"How's Nikki?" I asked as he led us into an attractively furnished den.

"Oh, she's mean as ever, you know her," he said, smiling. "Can I get you something to drink? Water, tea, coffee?" he asked, motioning for us to sit down.

"Coffee is good for me," I said, and Kelly said the same. He left to go prepare the coffee. Kelly said, looking around, "This place is beautiful."

Wallace returned with the coffee on a tray with cookies and condiments. After he sat down, I explained to Kelly that Nikki is Wallace's wife and that she is lead counsel for Sterling, Swarthmore, Beard, and Dauphine, a law firm with coast-to-coast and international reach.

"Is she around?" Kelly asked.

"No, unfortunately, she's at her sister's place in Taos," he explained. "She is dealing with a family estate thing and will be gone until Saturday."

"Ah, I see," I said.

"Yeah, well, she'll be upset that she missed you. We are going to see Cyrus in a couple of weeks, maybe on our way back, we can stop and see you and Callie," he said since we have already seen your brother Chase this year.

"How is she, anyway?" he asked.

"Good at this point, real good. That's a part of why we are here," I grimaced.

Kelly sat quietly as I explained everything about our case, including the call from Holtz and how I felt that he was involved in the disappearance of Uncle Jim and how the location relates to our case. Wallace sat quietly and listened until I finished, then stood and walked to a rear window that looked out to an expansive, well-manicured lawn bordered by native pines that varied.

"First, Holtz is one complicated bad guy. Secondly, he hated Jim, blamed him for his failed relationship with Callie, and for cutting him out of the business," he said, taking a sip of his coffee. "None of which is true. He's delusionally smart and vengeful," Wallace continued. Sitting down again and putting his cup on the tray, he asked, "How does he relate to your and Kelly's case?"

I then dropped what Ken uncovered and explained to me last night. This was the first time that Kelly heard this information too. Holtz Kovach works for Sys Tech Corporation as an executive; he's the V.P. of Security and Strategy. Her jaw dropped, and Wallace just smiled and shook his head.

"Let me tell you something about him: he's lethal and arrogant," Wallace explained to us. "So don't take him for granted. That's his strength and weakness. So, what's your next move?" he asked us.

"Well, we are going to meet a ranger who found Jim's wallet at the death scene of one of the victims in our case," I said, looking at my watch.

"What time is that supposed to happen?" he asked.

I explained that we have a meeting around three-thirty this afternoon, then we will return and get a hotel to stay in for the night and fly back to Cleveland tomorrow.

"Tell you what, you can stay here. We've got plenty of room," he insisted.

I asked if he was sure. We didn't want to impose, having already popped in quickly.

"Of course," he insisted, letting us know that it was nonsense for us to get a hotel. "It's a done deal. You're family," he finished.

"Is there anything else that you haven't told me yet?" Kelly questioned me.

"No," I said sheepishly.

"Parker, you thought someone was following you at the airport?" Wallace asked.

I explained about the person on the plane and seeing him again, paying quite a bit of attention to Kelly while I was taking care of the rental car.

"Well, I hardly see a problem with that. Kelly is quite stunning. Please excuse me for being forward," Wallace laughed. Kelly was blushing, but I could see she was still not happy with me.

"I agree, but the way he was observing us was more like studying us, taking notes," I said.

"Huh! Did you see anyone following you?" he asked.

"No... not really... Wait, there was a Tahoe, gray, that I noticed at the lake."

"Lake?... Oh, you mean the reservoir?" Wallace asked keenly.

"Yeah, I noticed it dropping back then... noticed it again when we got off at the exit," I said, shrugging.

He asked Kelly if she saw anything, and she said no but with the way things are going, she would not be surprised. Her attention was on the beautiful scenery.

"This is interesting, and I say you have to err on the side of caution." Standing, he signaled for us to follow him into his study. He was telling us as we followed him that Utah has an understanding gun law that supports the Second Amendment rights of law-abiding citizens. "Do you have your CCW?"

Chapter 63

Forty-five minutes was the time it took for us to finally arrive at Flaming Gorge National Recreation Area. This was after meeting with Ranger Whip Jordan at the Vernal Ranger District Office and getting a detailed map and GPS coordinates of the crime scene location. He didn't see a problem with us going out there to inspect; it was now an FBI matter for the most part.

"The crime scene has been processed as much as you can with mother nature adding changes daily and people walking over it," Whip's matter-of-fact response was.

He didn't put much stock in the fact that the crimes might be related or not; he just felt that those two climbers' deaths were unfortunate.

"We need to solve this, and fast, for the family's sake." Although from his point of view, the wallet was not there that long, it had to have been put there pretty recently.

"The FBI crime labs have the darn thing now; they said it is an open case... your uncle's, that is."

"Sorry you two came all the way out here to see that," he apologized. "Like I said to ole Raleigh... sorry, that's Raleigh Keith."

"He's the FBI agent in charge out from SLC. Those kids were executed, a hit. The person or persons knew what they were doing... and they knew the area quite well."

"That wallet was placed so that someone would no doubt find it. I'm just saying."

He paused for a moment to answer his ringing phone and was intently listening to the voice on the other end when my phone vibrated.

Looking down at the phone, I saw a text from Ken asking me to call him at my earliest convenience. This might be serious, I thought.

"Sorry about that, I'm going to have to cut this short. Got a call out on the other side of the gorge," Whip said, shaking his head and grinning. "It's always something going on up here."

"So you are related to Wallace and Nikki?" he asked.

"Yep, in an indirect kind of way," I laughed, thinking about those two.

"Good people! He makes a mean barbecue, and she makes the best margaritas this side of the Uintas," he said, standing and retrieving his gun from the desk. "If you go out there, be careful; it can get rugged off the path in some places and the rattlers..watch for em."

As we walked out, we shook hands, and he asked how long we were going to be here. I said about a day or two. Whip wished us good luck with the case and suggested a good restaurant for lunch. Leaving us in the parking lot, we decided to head up to Red Canyon Cove. The time was now a little after four, and the heat was on full blast.

Our drive up the two-lane Rt 191 was a mixed bag of green fields with cattle roaming and the brown, expansive view of cliffs, canyons, and rolling hills accented by the hue of evergreen with native pine trees. This, coupled with the gradually soaring height of the high Uintas mountains, presented an unforgettable treat to Kelly and me. I shared with Kelly that the actor James Woods and former OSU president E. Gordon Gee were from Vernal. We saw quite a few signs informing us about the Dinosaur National Monument, and she pointed out some bighorn sheep grazing along the road. Kelly checked my phone again. I had called Ken back, and he had not responded yet.

"Nothing yet. You want me to call MRO?" she asked, looking at me.

"Naw, time difference. It's almost eight," I replied, checking the rearview mirror. "There's a gray Tahoe following us," I informed Kelly as the road opened up on HWY 44, following a series of turns. The location we were now approaching was a panoramic, scenic, colorful landscape of painted rocky buttes, cliffs, canyons, and vistas of explosions of reds, yellows, and greens with a flowing, lively fluid of blue.

"Great...let's see what's what," she said, opening the glove box and removing the S&W M&P Shield 9mm, one of the two weapons that Wallace gave us for protection. Before we left the house, he suggested that we take some support in case we ran into some wild animals. The Shield, with a Crimson Trace green dot laser sight, was one, and a Glock 19 with an extra 15-round magazine was the other. Kelly was examining the Shield when I mentioned that we were now approaching our turnoff into the park. She stowed the gun back in the glove box and looked behind for the Tahoe.

I glided the Jeep between a Honda minivan and a Kia SUV at the parking area off the Mustang Ridge overlook and turned the car off. We sat there looking out the rearview mirror and the passenger side mirror. Kelly and I waited quietly to see if the gray Tahoe was going to pull into the lot. Two minutes later, it did and parked on the far side of the lot. Kelly had her hands on the glove box, ready to open it. My phone started to vibrate again. I looked down; it was a text.

A little boy chasing a little girl emerged from out of the brush to the west side of the Jeep, followed by two more screaming kids and a mom and dad. The doors of the gray Tahoe opened, and Kelly relaxed as two school-age girls stepped out of the rear and two older adults stepped out of the front. We looked at each other and smiled. The sun was still high in the sky, and it was hot.

"Well, let's get it on... time's a-wastin," I suggested, grabbing my phone and opening the door.

"We are here, and I am anxious to see what this place is all about," Kelly said, climbing out with me following, and we headed down N. Canyon Ridge Red Trail towards Red Rim Canyon Cove.

"Wow, it's unbelievably peaceful. You can see for miles," she said, staring out at the emerald blue water. We were standing right in the middle of the location where the terrible crime had taken place. You could see remnants of the crime scene tape where hikers had walked over it, and now discarded lengths hugged the brush. I looked at the location where Jim's wallet was found, and its proximity to where the bodies were located didn't make sense. I walked over and stood next to her and tried to enjoy the view, but my mind kept coming back to the same thing: what the hell was going on?

You could see the striations of different colors of the rocks and cliff faces as the sun reflected ghostly illuminations the lengths of the gorge, playing tricks with the hues that emitted from canyons and coves. What is blue to you and me is turquoise or azure to another, I thought, reaching for Kelly's hand. We sat down on a rock, holding hands, both wondering how someone could bring a horrendous crime to such a beautiful place and what the hell we were looking for.

We didn't say anything for a long period of time. She had been pretty quiet since Wallace's house; it must be wearing on her too.

People had been walking past us; everyone was friendly. I don't know how long we sat there, but the sun was starting to go down, and the light breeze we had earlier was picking up. The people that were hiking through had decreased; actually, I hadn't seen anyone for the last ten or so minutes. I checked my phone.

"Shit, we got problems," I said to Kelly.

Chapter 64

Tool had switched cars while the pair had been visiting. He didn't think that they would be going anywhere soon, so he called the rental car agency and asked for an exchange. No problem, they took care of it right away. His explanation was that it was more than he needed, so they gave him a sedan—a green Chrysler 200. Perfect, he thought. In and out within fifteen minutes, they had no clue he had even gone or was there for that matter. The burger and fries he had grabbed from the popular fast-food drive-through had hit the spot. Taking a pull from his water bottle, he followed as the two pulled into the parking lot of a popular hiking spot. Instead of turning in, he continued straight. The funny thing about this situation was that a vehicle like the one he initially had was two cars in front of him. He smiled at the irony of that, accelerating to the next exit and hitting the speed dial on his throwaway phone, Tool made a call.

"Tito, where are you at?" he asked.

"I'm close... and what did I tell you about that?" Tool said calmly, tightening his grip on the steering wheel. He really hated that guy.

Marcella laughed and said, "Oops! I forgot, buddy... ok, here's the deal. This is what we need..." He explained the plan and what he expected from Tool.

Jonas was just getting off the phone with the Europeans, who were a couple of hours outside of Green River and wanted to conclude the transaction this evening. He had arranged a meeting at ten that evening at a cabin located 12 miles south of Sys Tech R&D labs and 12 miles southeast of Green River off Flaming Gorge Pkwy. The cabin was a place that Jonas had known about from talking to other corporate managers before leaving good ole Ohio. He secured it before leaving and had scouted it out after arriving this morning. Nice, he thought. This was a precautionary measure in case things went south.

They all drove over together—Jonas, Paul Lee, and Marcella in the Range Rover and Doc with the other three men in the Jeep following—to check out the location. It was a half-mile gentle climb off the parkway, surrounded by a thick forested canopy of juniper pines and various mountain brush. This gave way to a mild downward left turn that opened up to a sweeping rise that leveled off to a spacious cabin with a turnaround drive.

The cabin was backed by the tree-covered slope of the foothills on both sides, as if the cabin was built in between a canyon. To the right, a stand of trees melted into a wooded opening as the rise gently fell to the banks of the Green River, which took a deviated right turn in its journey through the canyon walls.

Sleeping 14, with five bedrooms, four baths, and various other rooms looking out to an expansive view of the river and the wooded hillside beyond, it promoted a sense of desired seclusion.

Paul Lee and Marcella agreed with Jonas that this would work fine as the men climbed out of both vehicles. Marcella instructed the men to follow him and led them into the woods. Jonas and Paul Lee looked after the men, then unloaded two cases and their bags and carried them inside.

"Did you see the firepower that Marcella's crew had with them?" Paul Lee asked, setting down his bag and one of the hard cases.

"Hey, buddy, this is the big leagues. You can bet your Ivy League ass that our friends are packing," Jonas said, taking a bottle of Black Maple Hill bourbon from a well-stocked bar. "You got to love a rental company that deals only with corporate executives." Smiling, Jonas set down two glasses.

Marcella returned from the scouting trip and informed Jonas about the perimeter and what they have out there to deal with in case things go wrong with the visitors.

"What about the other problem?" Jonas asked Marcella.

"I have eyes on them. They will be making a visit to us, and you can deal with them in a short while," he said, smiling and pouring drinks for his guys. "My guy is pulling into the parking lot on those two right now."

Tool didn't like this, but they had doubled the money, and he wanted to get the rest of his cash, get the hell out of here, and be done with Marcella for good. Kill the bastard, he thought. Something to think about. Parking the car and grabbing a Beretta BU9 Nano out of the center console, he snorted, "This will do fine," and climbed out into the mild evening air.

Chapter 65

Holding Kelly's hand tightly and pulling her toward the parking lot, Parker was now looking around and wishing he had taken a gun with them. The text message might have come too late.

"Parker, what's going on?" Kelly asked, scared and looking behind them. He explained about the texts and that they were right to believe someone was following them because they were in the crosshairs. The air felt still, as if it was not moving, and although warm, the sweet mountain breeze was there. The sun was just starting its downward trajectory, casting a hazy orange-purple glow.

They reached the parking lot and found it empty of occupants, with the glow of taillights prematurely turned on by the leaving vehicles' auto light initiation systems, finding a dark area among the forested canopy of pine trees. Three vehicles remained: the Jeep, a brown Mini Cooper, and a green Chrysler sedan.

They walked quickly and purposefully to the Jeep. Kelly was about to climb in when, quietly and without raising suspicion, a man materialized from behind Parker with a gun pointed at the back of his head.

"Don't do anything stupid; I have no problem killing you."

"Now, very quickly, let's all get into your vehicle, and don't worry about the driver of this other car," he said in a slightly accented voice. "You first!" he said to Parker, then walked around to Kelly's side, keeping the gun trained on him. "Ok, lady, take this bag."

Kelly took the bag from his hand. It was pretty weighty.

"Let's move quickly, please. Put the bag in the back of the vehicle... quickly!"

Breathing out a puff of breath, he gestured with the gun as he said, "Hop in, lady, we have a drive."

"Dude, what do you want?" Parker asked after they were all in the car and the gun was still pointed at his head.

"Just drive, Parker, and try not to get killed. I'm in no mood," he said, tapping Parker on the neck.

Parker started to pull out of the parking lot, and the man said quietly, "Stop!" Then he pushed the button on the key fob to alarm the Chrysler. He reached into his shirt pocket and produced a cell phone.

"Program these directions into your unit," he said. Parker recognized the man as the one from the plane and the airport.

"Where are we going?" Parker asked.

He didn't answer, just kept the gun pointed at him and occasionally looked at Kelly.

"Who are you, and what do you want?" Kelly asked. He said nothing, just stared.

The GPS coordinates he gave Parker had them driving toward Dutch John, Utah.

"What the hell is going down?" Holtz said, stunned, as he watched through the scope while the pair and a third man got into the Jeep. The man was holding a gun on them and carrying a bag about the same size as his. He thought, oh boy! Fucking spoiler alert— someone was infringing on his plans, and this shit will not do. No, no, no!

He had known the bait was too good for Parker to resist, and just staking out the location would work. Holtz had planted a bug in Parker's home phone, so keeping track of his movements was not a problem. But now a new wrinkle was unfolding or had unfolded. He packed up his bag and was moving down the hill quickly, sliding, and at one point, he almost fell. They will have to come by this way based on the direction they turned leaving the parking lot.

"Shit, Holtz, my man, adapt... the party is on," he mumbled as he reached the parking lot and threw the bag into the back seat.

Chapter 66

The flight was pleasant enough. Agent Froom kept his newfound knowledge to himself, after spending three days at a Quantico seminar. He didn't boast about anything. Calfren found this quite odd and unsettling, and it made her worried. She had started going over notes about the West Branch, the Flaming Gorge, and the Bridgett Carlson killings, and to her astonishment, there was only one similarity: they were all shot. One was beaten up and raped, two were shot in the head, and two were shot in the heart, all with different calibers of weapons—two with a .380, one with a 9mm, and two with a .45.

The common denominator was they all worked for Sys Tech, a big government weapons developer.

If I may be so bold, she thought about saying this to her partner but thought better of it. Smiling instead, she turned in her seat, adjusting her glasses, and said to Froom, "My gut tells me that Sys Tech is at the core of these killings. Any thoughts?"

"Yep! We interviewed the CEO and the VP of Corporate Security or something. They were vague and deflected everything," Froom agreed. "They were hiding something. HR had nothing to say, but the generic good things about the employees," he finished. "They have a big project with the government. Odd thing, no one wants to talk about it. You know those people knew something. The guy worked on a new top-secret project." He turned to face her and pointed at a name on the report she was reading.

"He's been untouchable, and now he's up in Green River, Wyoming," she turned the page. "And... MRO... I mean Parker, is up there with a client, one of the victims' sisters. Geez, this is not going to be good if it's what I think." He shrugged, holding his hands out.

"When we land, there should be a car for us. I'll call Agent Keith and Ranger Whip Jordan," she thought, rubbing her temples. Damn! He's never made that much sense before, she stared at him. What the hell happened to him down at Quantico? Stranger things have happened, she thought.

Agent Froom pointed out, "We better call Ken Roberts at MRO. There's something they are not telling us!"

"You are right," Cafren thought. Damn, another productive suggestion from the new Froom.

Parker continued driving, knowing that they had two guns in the car. Hopefully, he doesn't look in the glove box; his was under the driver's seat. "How much further?" he asked, trying to make conversation and looking at Kelly in the rearview mirror. She looked exhausted, but she smiled back, looking intensely focused.

"Are you going to say anything, at least tell us why you're doing this?"

To their surprise, he answered, "Apparently, you know or have something they want," he said matter-of-factly. Parker was hoping for a state highway patrol to pull them over. He had slowly started to speed up over the last few miles and drift into the other lane. The man noticed.

"You might want to slow down a bit," he said, pointing with the gun and checking his seat belt tightness. "Why don't you tell me?" he asked.

"Tell you what?" Parker looked at him and then back at the road.

"What these assholes want from you two, they are paying me a lot," he said. Apparently, he didn't appreciate his employers. Parker might be able to use this to their advantage.

"To bring you to them," Tool finished.

"A thumb drive," Kelly said quickly.

"Ah, what's on it?" Tool smiled.

"Incriminating pictures of men meeting with each other," Parker said. This little tidbit was interesting, Tool thought, and turned to look out the passenger window. Parker caught Kelly's attention again in the mirror, and she was trying to communicate with her eyes. Parker understood that Tool didn't know, and maybe they could use this to their advantage. At least he hoped that's what he understood.

His phone vibrating broke the hypnotic, repetitive whirling of the Jeep's tires. It was full-on dark now as the last glint of the sun crept behind the massive shoulders of the Uintas to the west.

"Yes, I have them. They are alive, of course. Do you have my money?" Tool listened for what seemed like a long time, but was really only seconds before responding, "Wyoming now, do what?!"

"Yeah, just saw the sign. We are in Wyoming and now double back to Utah, I guess." A knot was forming in Parker's stomach. He had no idea who these people were and how they would get out of this shit, but he promised that he would for Kelly's sake.

"Turn up here and follow the road," Tool said.

Both sides of the two-lane road were wide-open fields devoid of color, just dark obstructions representing the ebb and flow of the hillsides scrubbed with brush rising into the rock butte and distant mountain ranges.

"Who are these people and why Wyoming and now back to Utah?" Parker asked.

"Have you heard of Sys Tech?"

"It's them. They want you. Where's the thumb drive?" Tool asked, looking at Kelly, gun still pointed at Parker.

Parker looked in the rearview mirror and saw the same set of headlights that had been following them since Dutch John, Utah. "It's in my bag with the computer."

Tool's mind was now racing, thinking that this could be a double-cross, a trap. Marcella would have the upper hand with his men there. Surely it would have been foolish not to have considered this the whole time. This damn job has been kind of odd from the inception. What was so important about the thumb drive, and how much money was it worth to them?

"Pull over and stop here!" he demanded.

They were at the mouth of a drive surrounded by trees on both sides that seemed to rise. The car behind them had closed the distance so fast that Parker could feel the heat from its light beams penetrating the dead still night air surrounding the car.

Chapter 67

All kinds of scenarios were playing in and out of Holtz's mind as he caught up to Parker's Jeep while they sped by Dutch John. He just didn't need a pronghorn antelope or a deer to run out in front of him as he was singing an old song by Social D, "Bad Luck."

"Thirteen's my lucky number..." he was crooning as he saw the Jeep pulling to the side of the road up ahead. Holtz moved over to the opposite lane and went around, noticing a driveway to the right disappearing up into a forested climb. He continued around to the next bend, about an eighth of a mile, and pulled over into what looked to be another driveway. Turning off the lights, he sat there to the count of one hundred, then quietly climbed out of the car, opened the rear door, and grabbed a flashlight out of the bag. By the time he walked back up around the bend cautiously through the ditch, the car was gone.

"Shit!" he whispered.

Thinking analytically and walking back to his car, Holtz quickly realized the car had gone up the driveway. He knew this area as well as anyone, so he would take this driveway and parallel them. Pulling out his GPS, he triangulated his location and knew what he was going to do.

"Pull in front of the white car and park facing out," Tool said to Parker, watching the cabin's front door.

Parker did this as a group of men unfolded themselves from the cabin and started walking toward them.

Tool told Parker to get out of the car first and leave the keys on the floor. As he did, Kelly said, "Crap, Parker, look..." She recognized three of the men in the group approaching them.

"Damn..." Parker whispered to Kelly as she walked up close and leaned into him.

Tool continued pointing the gun at them, never wavering, with distaste on his face for the approaching group of men.

"Tito, my cuz, you never disappoint... never... never... did they give you a hard time?" one of the men said, smiling and patting Tool on the back. He had a closely shaved head and a megawatt smile.

"That's the bitch who did this to my eye." A man we recognized walked over quickly, stood in front of us, and with lightning speed, slapped Kelly. The blow caused Kelly to fall back against me.

I braced her to keep her from falling to the ground as the man reached back to hit her again.

It was as if an explosion of heat and fire rocked that precise moment in time. I felt the crunch of bone, the sticky wetness of blood, and hands grabbing me, pulling me back.

"Gentlemen, gentlemen!... now, now....!" The shaved-head man was speaking as two men grabbed my arms. I was standing over the bloodied body of the man who hit Kelly. His nose was gushing blood, and he was not moving. "Damn, Parker! You... my friend, have, umm... anger issues..." The man with the shaved head was smiling, standing over and looking down at the bloody man on the ground.

The man who brought us to them had moved slowly during the excitement, and now his position had angled to be able to cover all of the parties standing in the driveway. Something was up, and it looked like the man named Tito did not trust these people.

"Marcella, what's going on... man?"

A voice was coming from up on the deck. Parker looked up and saw two other men standing on the deck with drinks in their hands, looking down.

"Bring in the company, guys... whew boys, where's your manners!" Marcella barked, pointing at the guy on the ground. "Wake his ass up."

The guy holding me released his grasp. I recognized him from Kelly's house. Turning to us, the tall man named Marcella said, "Please..." and gestured for us to follow him into the cabin. I grabbed Kelly.

As we walked up the steps with Tito behind us, I heard one of the two men say, "He got knocked the fuck out..." and laugh.

Chapter 68

Holtz followed the road south for a quarter of a mile to a point where it turned back on itself and headed west towards what his GPS showed was the road Parker had gone down. He was now on foot, having followed the river upstream for ten minutes to what looked like a cabin. He had not encountered any wildlife, although he did hear the occasional scurrying through the woods but no animals out hunting. The trek was not a problem, having done much worse as an Army Ranger; this was a cakewalk. He was now positioned 300 meters downstream from the cabin, up on the side of a hill in a recess that afforded a great overlook and the camouflage of the trees, as well as an escape route down the river to his vehicle. The other route would have him going up over the ridge behind his location—a not-so-easy climb but doable.

Holtz opened up the backpack and removed a night vision sighting scope, a second flashlight with a red filter, and a pair of night vision goggles. He had come prepared to stay overnight if necessary. His pack contained food, water, a sleeping bag, a jacket (which he put on now), and most importantly, his weapons. Holtz had no idea who else was in the cabin besides Parker and the woman, Kelly. Although he had his suspicions, he was not sure of the other players, so he felt it was important to find out what was going on. This meant a closer inspection. Damn, he loved this shit—the hunt.

With faint moonlight and the river to guide himself upstream, he grabbed a hunting knife out of the pack and his S&W M&P 9L. He put the night vision goggles on his head and down-climbed to the river. Coming up on the east side of the cabin, Holtz was afforded a nice view into one of the cabin's huge glass windows. After sneaking up the rear side steps, he just sat there and listened. Thank God these men had no idea how to secure a location—they were just city thugs. Holtz was quite surprised to see Jonas and Paul Lee in the room interrogating Parker and Kelly. This whole shit storm was about Jonas and Paul Lee selling the S.M.A.R.T. to some Europeans who were en route to this location.

Bullshit, he thought. It was safe to assume that they were behind three of the killings, and hell, we know who did the other two, he smiled and whispered. "Well, old boy, not your problem."

Parker was sitting in a chair with the woman next to him and an open laptop on the table. The woman had a black eye. Parker, poor boy, was bleeding from the nose and mouth and looked worse for wear. Holtz smiled, noticing that Paul Lee and a tall bald man kept looking at their watches.

There was a guy standing, looking disinterested, with a gun trained on the prisoners, and three other guys scattered around the room checking weapons.

Jonas answered his phone and started talking. Everyone in the room stopped what they were doing and watched him. "Okay, they are close and will be here in ten," he said. Two of the men on the couch got up and moved towards the door and stopped. The bored one with the gun asked the bald guy a question and didn't look pleased with the answer.

Time to go. Moving quietly and stealthily off the deck back down the river to his perch, Holtz had some planning and thinking to do after what he had just seen and heard.

Chapter 69

Parker saw the first of the three blows and was able to move and deflect the punch, but on the fourth one, he couldn't move his head fast enough and felt the punch land square on his jaw. A guy named Jonas, a Sys Tech bigwig, was directing the beatdown by his hired man, Marcella.

"Is this the only copy of the thumb drive?" Marcella asked, looking over at Jonas and another man named Paul Lee, another bigwig at Sys Tech.

"Smack the girl gently," Jonas said as if this was a game. Marcella looked at him as if to say, "You gotta be kidding, right?" One of the other guys sitting on the couch said, "I've got an idea. Why don't we bring Smitts in? He would love to see the girl."

They laughed, and Marcella mentioned to the group what had happened at the first encounter at Kelly's house a few days ago, with Smitts getting hit in the head with the laptop. They laughed some more, except the man named Tito, who still had a gun trained on them.

Marcella and Tito were not agreeing about something. When we first entered the cabin, Marcella asked him a question, and Tito said, "Finish the job!" and called him Tito. Tito replied, "I've told you for the last time, don't call me that."

Marcella was back in front of them again, this time standing in front of Kelly, forcing her legs apart and reaching over to stroke her hair. He grinned at Parker and said, "You know, dude, you have a very, very pretty girlfriend here. Too bad for you, though..."

"I am going to wear those long legs out and then pass her around to all the boys here, including 'BIG' Smitt..." He smiled, yanking hard, pulling her head back, and kissing her throat.

Kelly resisted, and he let go and smacked her on the back of the head. "Bitch!" he said again, laughing.

Raising my head and spitting out blood, I smiled and said, "I'm going to kill you, cue ball."

I was rewarded with a hard right that glanced off my forehead, knocking me over in the chair and bouncing my head off the floor.

"What's that, Parker? Parker, what's that?" Marcella got down on the floor to talk to me, putting his face right next to mine. Just a little closer, you fuck, and I will bite your nose off.

He didn't; instead, he grabbed me by the hair, sat me up, and turned his attention to Kelly again.

"She just doesn't know yet that this guy standing in front of her... killed her brother and that little girl back in Ravenna..." he said. "Ain't that right, Tito? Damn, I mean Tool. Sorry, old habits are hard to break, cuz. Just a contract kill."

Kelly was shocked and confused, tears welling up in her eyes as she thought of these people responsible for Guy's death.

"Marcella, you are an evil dude. Please film it if possible, like the girl in PA..." Jonas said, taking a drink from his whiskey and sitting down.

They laughed again, but Tito did not. He just stared and kept pointing the gun.

Marcella turned to Parker and moved in his direction. "Parker, you will watch and love it. The thing about me is, I could kill you in the morning and be out dancing salsa in the evening..." He did a little salsa move, which caused a couple of guys to laugh.

"You're a dead piece of shit," Parker spat blood out as he and Marcella stared each other down. He was about to punch me again when Jonas's phone vibrated, and they all looked in his direction.

"Yes, okay, you have the location," Jonas was saying into the phone. I wasn't paying attention to what he shouted to the guys in the room. I reached over and touched Kelly's finger. She touched mine, looked at me, and smiled. I winked and pointed at a severely pissed Tito. The two guys on the couch, Jimmy Doc and some young guy named Marko Blanks, jumped up and grabbed their weapons—an Ithaca 12 gauge shotgun and an M&P 40 for Doc, and a SIG Sauer P228 with a Viridiax laser sight for Marko.

Parker thought, damn, some power for the European buddies.

"So where is my money? I didn't sign up for the rest of this shit, Marcella. I would like my cash," Tito was saying as the other two guys stopped at the door.

"You will get it after we make the exchange. Trust me, cuz," Marcella smiled and looked at Jonas, who was opening a case with two strange-looking handheld 7x5 inch flat screens and something that looked slightly larger than a wristwatch.

"What should we do with these two?" Paul Lee was asking Jonas as Marcella instructed his men.

"Tell Slim to come down... and I need you to come over here pronto," he said to Marko. "Tito, I'm sorry... I mean Tool, could you go up high and keep watch?"

"Did you bring that badass mutha with you?" Marcella asked.

"It's what you're paying for, right?" he said.

"Good... Doc, take him to the spot."

Kelly and I were sitting there taking all of this in when Marko walked over and slapped me in the head and said, "You dead... BITCH!"

My head was spinning, but I could make out what Jonas told Marcella. Good, an opportunity is all we need.

"Take them out to the storage shed and tie them up. We'll deal with them later, after the company is gone," Jonas had commanded.

Marcella called Marko over and instructed him on what to do with us. I thought, here we go.

The time was now if we were going to save ourselves. Marko had recruited a still-dazed Slim at the request of Marcella. This would hopefully work to our advantage. Marko was not the brightest bulb in the box, and his young bravado and lack of experience in the woods would help. Slim was still dazed; he looked concussed. I could see this in his demeanor. He held the gun loosely at Kelly's back, and his movements were sluggish. They marched us out back and up the walkway.

God bless the owners or whoever built this house, because the shed was not right next to the house.

Chapter 70

It happened very fast. The pathway leading up the hillside into the cover of the forest was no more than four feet at its widest point and very uneven. Whatever they kept in the shed couldn't have been large or heavy because it would have been difficult to get it down to the cabin. Fifty yards up the hill, isolated from the cabin's view, I saw the headlights of a car as it parked in front of the cabin and saw the shadowed figures of five occupants as they emerged.

"Move your punk ass..." Marko sang. He was behind me, prodding me with the gun at the small of my back.

"How you doing, Slim?" he asked, breathing hard as the altitude affected him.

Kelly was in the front with the flashlight, marching up the path. Slim was stumbling behind her, gun pointed down, pushing her. The only response was breathing and grunting.

"Hey, Parker, are there rattlers out here?" Marko asked me as we reached the motionless darkness of the tree line.

Thirty yards to go. I didn't answer.

"Hey, asshole, are there snakes out here?" he asked again.

"Yes, and mountain lions, bears, and coyotes..." I said, hoping to distract him with our conversation.

"Shit, here? all of them, here around us rattlers on the ground, here?" He stopped, looking into the thick blackness.

Kelly and Slim were about twenty-five yards from the shed's level surface and its forested cover.

"Hey, Slim... stop," Marko said.

Kelly had the flashlight's beam concentrated on the path's uneven, rocky dirt surface when Marko's hushed voice cut through the muted footfalls of the four. Up until this point, Slim had not spoken a word. I could see that he was in bad shape as he struggled up the weather-worn path. Turning around, he was in the process of saying, "What?" when the flashlight beam made an unusual sweeping arc that connected with a familiar thud. Marko was directly behind me, bent over and sucking in air, when I whirled and caught him with a backhand fist to the jaw, dropping him like a sack of potatoes. The momentum of the swing carried us both backward, with me landing on top as we toppled down the trail. I scrambled around with my left hand, reaching for the gun, and my two fingers came to rest inside the trigger guard behind the trigger. His wrist was bent back at an odd angle. I hit him once in the head as he tried to wrestle me off, pushing his open palm into my face. With my right hand swatting at his hand, my right knee made contact with his groin.

The guy was pretty quick and tried to turn sideways, but I outweighed him by fifty pounds. He let out a momentary groan and moved his hand from my face, trying to punch up at my head. It was too late. Using all of my weight, I dropped and swung my elbow into the side of his head. I felt a shuddering bump; he was out before he knew it. Struggling up, I found Kelly crawling backward from under a pine tree, holding up Slim's pistol and the flashlight. She was smiling.

Slim's body was lying half under a tree, with his legs resting twisted upward on the trail.

"You are good," I whispered, looking back down at the cabin as I reached down and pulled Marko's shoes off, throwing them downslope toward the river.

Kelly walked over, put her arms around me, and hugged me, burying her head in my chest. I kissed the top of her head and held her tight.

"I thought we were going to die here," she said, looking up at me with tears in her eyes. "That guy killed my brother. Did you hear what they said? That Tool, Tito murderer, killed Guy and Laurie for them. Parker, he did it..." She cried.

"Yeah, I know. We'll get him, but right now we've got to get out of here," I said, going through Marko's pockets and retrieving his phone. "Too many people with guns down by the cars, plus we are blocked in."

A voice called out from the cabin for Marko and Slim. At the same time, both of their phones started vibrating. A light was coming out of the back of the cabin and headed up the trail. Then a gunshot rang out from the dark of night.

"Let's go this way." I grabbed Kelly's arm as two more shots whizzed by.

Chapter 71

Psst... Psst... Two more shots whizzed by them as they dropped down to the river's edge and hid behind two large boulders. Kelly had Slim's Beretta Px4 Storm with a dual-beam laser flashlight mounted to it, and I had Marko's P226, good for the close kill. We were just about 200 yards downstream from the cabin, making our way back up the hill when we heard more men behind us. We had to keep the flashlight's glow down, so the going was very slow. Two shots pinged off the rocks on the other side of the river; thank God they were not good shots.

"We've got to make it back up to that rise and double back towards the cabin and try to get to the road or find another house," I said. The forest cover was good and dense with the healthy growth of pine trees in the mountain terra firma. Three shots rang out in succession, and I heard the unmistakable cry of one man being hit, and these shots were not coming from behind us; they were off to the side.

I tapped Kelly on the shoulder. "Let's go there," I pointed, and we ran hard and low.

Holtz was tracking the two of them through the illumination of his PNC x200 Tactical thermal night vision scope when he first decided that this would be just as good a place as any to kill Parker and his little girlfriend Kelly Ryan. But then he saw Jonas and Paul Lee out meeting the Ukrainian group in front of the cabin, and his attention was drawn to them as they greeted each other and then disappeared inside. Just before they showed up, another man left the cabin carrying an unmistakable bag, disappearing into the treeline across from the driveway in direct line of sight of Holtz. He knew what was inside a bag like that. This guy was a contract guy like himself, but who? And working for Jonas. Holtz figured that this guy must have done the West Branch killing for Jonas; it made sense. The guy was an engineer who worked on that project for Jonas. Training his sight back on Parker and Kelly, Holtz was treated to a new scenario. Those two had overpowered their captors and now were back in his crosshairs.

He squeezed off two more rounds, missing on purpose.

"Well, the fly said to the spider..." He was saying as he looked through the scope, watching one of the men climbing among the boulders, pitched backwards. "Damn, wasn't me," he smirked, training his weapon back on the large picture window at the cabin and pulling the trigger.

"This is turning into a cluster fuck, and I gotta get out... but let's have a little fun."

"Your lucky day, Parker! Wooohooo!"

Chapter 72

We ran from the cover of the forest, traversing an opening, hiding behind a boulder, and quickly doubled back on an upslope trajectory. Running for the treeline again, low and hard, and praying... I could hear the men crashing through the woods as they got closer. I don't think they realize that we have the two downed thugs' guns.

Four shots pierced through the air, exploding off the boulders, spewing sparking shards into the darkening night sky. Kelly was in front of me, in the shadow of the wood line. We were above and west of the cabin slightly, having doubled back twice along the river. I could see the glow of the cabin's lights faintly as they illuminated the dark, shadowless woods. The moon cast a hollow glow that helped as well as hindered. Turning around and sheltering myself between the massive branches of a pine tree, I aimed as I saw two figures emerge, coming up the hill right at the forest line, and quickly squeezed off three rounds at what I thought was the center mass on both. The weapon moved slightly in my hand as the shots hit home. A large, hulking figure with a small head howled and lurched backward in the pale light of the moon.

The smaller of the two screamed, stumbled down, and was trying to crawl back toward the cover of a large pine tree. I turned, breathing hard and feeling like my lungs were about to explode, as shots were exploding in front and to the side of me. The earth gave out, and I was falling.

Kelly was under the forest cover as the two men came out of the woods firing at Parker. He was too close to the edge of the hillside, still in the woods but exposed if you were coming directly at him, she thought, readying her gun to fire. She noticed that he had taken refuge under the branches of a large tree, but he was still too close to the edge. The men were down, then the shots started. She turned to take cover and was down; the last thing she saw was Parker going over the edge, and she screamed.

The pain resonated from my left side in arcs. I was wedged against a fallen tree where my tumbling came to a stop twenty-five feet down the mountain. I remained motionless long enough to remember what happened. I was knocked backward and was tumbling out of control, trying to stop, and then blackness.

Okay, I painfully pulled myself from against the tree and scrambled forward and up toward a small cavity surrounded by a grouping of small pine trees. Phsst.. phsst.. two more shots high above the branches in the trees. I was thinking of Kelly as my confusion started to clear. The glow of the interior lights radiated across the rear deck and up the slope. The road was another sixty yards to the right of me. I looked up, and it was eerily quiet, and then three shots kicked up the dirt to the right of me, then four more head high, hitting the tree to my left. He was toying with me.

"Shit!" I said, and then all hell broke loose. Shots were going all through the cabin; I could hear windows breaking, men screaming. The shots were coming from the southeast and the west. It seemed like the mountain's night air was ringing with gunfire.

Standing, I was worried about Kelly up there and saw that I was about forty yards west of the cabin's rear.

I had fallen simply down the slope after tripping over a tree root as the gunfire erupted.

Looking straight ahead upslope, the target objective in my mind now! I fired off a double tap in each direction of where I imagined the shots came from and ran. The blood was pumping in my head as I took the first step, clumsily stumbling upward and then noisily staying as low as my six feet two height would allow. I moved my arms thrashing past the small tree stumps, up the slope zigzagging, clawing, foot smashing against rocks, roots, and downed tree fall, grunting under branches until I made it over the top, falling. It wasn't until then that I realized that no one was shooting at me as I ran up across the hillside, kneeling, breathing hard, trying to focus into the opaque darkness. "Shit," I huffed out.

"Kell, Kelly," I said in a hushed tone. It was silent except for the sounds of the woods for what seemed like minutes. "Over here, I'm over here," she said in an exhausted breath.

I stood, stumbling, and struggled to see in the darkened woods. "Where?"

I found her pinned by two massive branches from a subalpine fir pine tree that were shot off from the hail of bullets. "You okay?" I hurried to get them off her. "Yes, I think so... just please hurry."

As I removed the last branch, swatting at mosquitoes, I heard the unmistakable sound of a car door closing and driving up the driveway and the distant wail of sirens. Helping her up, she asked me, "Are there really rattlesnakes and mountain lions out here..."

"Yep, and I saw one back on the trail... dead though."

I could see she was scratched up and limping, but she was still holding the gun.

"Think I will need this?" She asked.

"I hope not, I certainly hope not," I said, kissing her on the lips and walking out.

Chapter 73

I was never so happy to be back home in the CLE or suburban Westlake. The weather, well, let's just say that it's not raining, but it's still hot as hell for September. Kelly and I stayed that night in Vernal after the Daggett County Sheriff Department, who arrived on the scene first, followed by the FBI, finished their interviews. It was Wallace who called a friend in the Sheriff department when he couldn't get a hold of us and started to worry. This led to multiple calls to MRO and information being exchanged about the case, coupled with neighbors of the cabin owners who live on the other side of Rt 191 seeing suspicious people in the area and the gunfire.

The Sheriff Department was able to get the rental car agency to give them the location of our vehicle without a subpoena or search warrant; all of the cars have GPS locators on them, so they were able to triangulate the location. FBI agents Cafren O'Malley and Kenneth Froom were en route to Vernal to meet with Ranger Whip Jordan when she got her call back from Ken. He explained to her that Parker might be in trouble based on information squeezed from one of Marcella's men from the airport attack. They had a file on Marcella and knew that he had a longstanding relationship with Jonas.

How in-depth of a file, we have no idea yet. Nothing stuck out except that the two were from Baltimore and worked on some charities together. They knew that Marcella was a businessman and that he was linked to successful import/export businesses in Ohio City and Baltimore, Maryland. Ranger Jordan had just returned from a call in the field and got a call from the Sheriff's department as the FBI arrived; he alerted them to the situation. Kelly and I had walked down to the road and sat down in front of the opening to the cabin's driveway on the side of the hill; we threw our weapons onto the other side of the road and put our hands behind our heads as the first cruiser came down. I was explaining this to everyone in the conference room when Kelly walked in. I walked over and hugged her, kissed her.

"You want coffee or tea?" I asked her as everyone said hello and she sat down.

"I'll have what you got," she said, looking very tired and sporting the black eye and a few more scratches. "So did you guys go back into the house?" Styles asked, getting up to grab another coke.

"Ooooh..." Kelly winced.

"Yeah!" I said and licked my lips and continued. After the Sheriff cleared us, thanks to Cafren and Whip, we walked back over toward the front where we had our Jeep and the two other vehicles parked. I explained to the Sheriff and Cafren about the location up the hillside where I shot at two of our pursuers; he sent two men up to that location. I paused and took a deep breath, looking at Kelly, and explained the carnage. Two bodies were found in front of the Tahoe, multiple shots to the bodies and each had a head wound. The body position suggested they were trying to leave when they were shot. Inside the cabin was a bloodbath; five bodies, each person had head wounds and multiple shots. Some of the wounds were after the guys were down. It was an execution, a carefully orchestrated hit or something, Parker said. Cafren called it that, and the sheriff looked at her, said, "Let's not jump to any conclusions." "Look, it was bad there in Green River, it was bad," he continued.

Two more bodies were found downstream about sixty yards; they only had two wounds.

Parker remembered the men chasing them and then hearing the shots.

He looked at Kelly, "Those shots might have saved us," Parker recounted.

She remembered too, thinking that someone was looking out for them, and they had an idea who it might have been. At that point, the sheriff didn't know about the whole situation, Parker said.

"I couldn't handle it, so I went back to the car," Kelly said. "Yeah, it was bad," Parker replied as Ken got up to see who had just come in. They could hear footfalls on the steps, and in walked Agent O'Malley and Agent Froom; everyone exchanged greetings.

"Agents, would you like something to drink?" Callie asked them. Cafren said that coffee would be fine; Agent Froom settled on a cup of tea. They sat down and wanted to share some updates and explained to the MRO staff that the Office of Homeland Security and the DOJ were handling the investigation now because of the international interest from the dead men not being US citizens.

The three Albanians and two Ukrainians were in the country legally, but they did have terrorist ties.

"We are still providing support," Agent Froom sneered, and Cafren turned and frowned at him.

She explained what happened that night in Ashley National Forest and how it's reverberating across the political landscape. Eleven people were found shot, five Europeans, six Americans. Nine of the victims were shot with high-velocity rounds from a sniper weapon. Five of the nine were shot with a .375 caliber round from possibly a CheyTac M200, and the other four were shot with ammunition that was a .408 caliber. That could be a number of weapons, and based on the size of the bag your kidnapper had with him, we are sure he was, in fact, one of the snipers.

In fact, all seven in the cabin were cut to pieces by serious high-tech weapons, two to be exact.

The other four were shot with a nine-millimeter; one survived, lucky us," she rolled her eyes.

"The guy can almost make up his own story about the events," she mused.

"Parker, you are cleared of any crimes," she pointed out quickly.

"Right now, pertaining to the men you shot, one died, and one survived," she said.

"Kelly, I'm sorry about your brother."

"The survivor, Jimmy "Doc" Donovan, talked and helped piece some things together," Cafren said.

She continued to explain how Guy helped to develop a weapon for Sys Tech that was part of a new Direct Energy Weapons initiative. This weapon was funded by congressional support and some house bills that were, in part, an item of special interest by former Senator Mirack and other members of the House Armed Service Committees. She explained how it would be quite hard to really know all of the players at the moment. But the former Senator was/is, it's kinda murky right now, a board member of Sys Tech. Jonas Habbas and Paul Lee Raverstine, whose bodies were found with the others in Utah, are dead, orchestrated the killing with the help of Marcella from Sys Tech Corporate location. Their bank records are under scrutiny as we speak. There was no money found at the crime scene, but again, resources have said that two cases containing a large amount of cash were there and have not been found yet.

We are assuming that one or both of the shooters took these cases. We know the name of one of the alleged shooters, and he is alleged to be the triggerman named Tito or The Tool in the Guy Ryan and Laurie Rice murders. The Bridgett Carlson murder was at the hand of Marcella Lopez as well, and Parker's and Kelly's kidnapping was his idea, which was carried out by Tool too. We are still at odds on the identity of the other shooter at the Utah location and the murder of Jim Rice and Rebecca Richman. She finished with, "Glad you folks are okay," and tells Parker, "Please, please don't do this again."

"Oh! the wallet had nothing to do with these crimes...at least directly..." she said. "That!we are still working on." If there are any updates, which I am sure there are because of the nature of this situation, I will be keeping you all informed. Please do not talk to the press; this is an active investigation. Parker, Kelly, we are really glad that you are okay; I don't have to tell you how bad it could have been.

Chapter 74

Parker was reclining in the tub with Kelly sitting between his legs as the steam settled around them. He took a sip of his Jefferson's Bourbon and thought about how good this moment felt; the smooth burn of its sweet, dark, smoky flavor relaxed his bruised and battered body. Not to be outdone in the healing process, Kelly's presence was the number one reason he felt so at ease. Kelly splashed him with water and said, "You look too content, and I haven't done anything."

They had taken a few days of relaxation and went to the Finger Lakes Region in upstate NY for some hiking and biking. Guy's funeral was the last of the people killed a week ago, and it was time for some healing. "No, I was just thinking that the moment was perfect," Parker said, smiling. She took a drink of wine and said, "Not as perfect as it will be later," and kissed him hard on the lips. The case was out of our hands, and life was back to normal at MRO, crazy as hell for some and not so for others; there was still work to be done.

Hours and miles away in Albemarle County, VA, the Mercedes SUV lazily drove down a lonely tree-lined backcountry road twenty-six miles from Charlottesville. It was a perfect late summer, early fall day to be out for a drive in Virginia horse country. Stately horse farms dotted both sides of the newly paved road. The unmarked driveway was just ahead; the historical home of 11,000 square feet sat up on a small rise surrounded by 125 acres of prime equestrian real estate.

With its spectacular equestrian facilities, barns, and equipment buildings, it alone was breathtaking. A man was standing under the covered porch of the southern plantation-style house. He was older and dressed impeccably in a suit; he approached the car as it parked. "Please follow me, sir; he is waiting for you in the library," he spoke in a commanding tone. Nothing else was spoken, and the man followed him into the magnificent house.

"It's good to see you; how was your trip?" a tall, handsomely dressed man asked as the other man entered a very elegant and well-furnished library. "It was good, very productive," the man responded.

"Bourbon?" he was asked by the man getting up from a dark cherry leather couch and walking over to a corner bar. He poured two generous tumblers of the fine dark liquor and handed one to the other gentleman. Both men sat back down on the couch, each taking a long sip and appreciatively nodding.

The phone rang twice, and then it was picked up. "Hello, Senator, it's me... you have a cluster fuck."

www.ingramcontent.com/pod-product-compliance
Lightning Source LLC
Chambersburg PA
CBHW062119020426
42335CB00013B/1019